To *m* ...

You *will* *always*

be *my* *hero.*

Niels

&

Johanne

from

DENMARK

Jimmy

by James Bjorn Thordahl

Aventine Press

Published by Aventine Press
1023 4th Ave #204
San Diego CA, 92101
www.aventinepress.com

ISBN: 1-59330-474-9

Library of Congress Control Number: 2007928576
Library of Congress Cataloging-in-Publication Data
Niels & Johanne from Denmark

Printed in the United States of America

For:
Jacob Bjorn,
    Kyle Bjorn,
        and Riley Dane.

    Grand Grandsons—All.

Contents

Introduction

This is the story of a Danish man and woman, not so young when they met, who, after leaving their home country, married, immigrated to America, and raised a family of eight children in a rural environment at a time of great world despair. It includes a few somewhat relevant stories from their seventh child. I was their seventh child. Although their views may provide a different perspective, I believe my memories and experiences could be those of any of the eight Thordahl children.

I have not been alone in writing this tribute to our parents. The Bjørn family reunions triggered some memories as I listened to stories from my siblings and others. Sherri Twente, my niece, collected the memories of the eight children for the first of our Thordahl family reunions, in 2005. I have drawn heartily from their recollections to tell Niels and Johanne's story.

Hopefully, my stories portray what life was like in their time. Too late in life I questioned what their early life was like and what they may have wished us to know of other facets of their life. Where my stories present the story of my early life, my story can somewhat be their story too. Family history is so easily lost when it is not adequately recorded. With this book I hope to begin the recording of my family's history and urge all to record in some media their family history.

To overcome "writers block," I began to participate in a group which was dedicated to writing autobiographies. Hearing the members' short stories bimonthly instilled a focus toward continual progress in documenting my life story, encouraged a willingness to share my stories, and nourished a desire to make some of them entertaining. In this book, I wish to include all the relative stories that I have written or collected in a tribute to our parents, Niels and Johanne. Remembering that my stories were autobiographic initially, I wish the reader to see me only in the background. Choosing to be in the background would be true to my nature.

Some of my stories originally talked to my descendants, or to my siblings, in honor of them, or to other family members, and some stories talked to the members in the writing group. I may have wished only to entertain in one, inform in another, or document a profound life experience. The reader is left to decide what to take from each.

Most of my writing is raw storytelling for the sake of getting these stories documented. To make each story understandable and readable without orally struggling, I read many stories to my wife, Bonnie. I greatly appreciate her willingness to listen and provide valuable suggestions, and I do not transfer any responsibility for lack of quality in my effort. I am deeply indebted to a new acquaintance and greatly appreciated friend, Beverli Jinn, who kindly and professionally provided grammatical correction and editorial evaluation. I most sincerely thank Reverend Paul L. Peck, the leader of our autobiography writing group, who so generously gives of his time, his wisdom, his guidance and encouragement so others may be inspired to achieve their goals. I am so grateful that he also reviewed my text and provided personal recommendations.

Most of the pictures were provided to me by my brothers and sisters. Further information regarding the pictures is included in the Index of Pictures.

In all of this effort I, alone, am responsible for any grammatical errors and inaccuracies of facts.

To the readers in Denmark (I hope there will be some.): I offer this book as a connection to fellow family descendants, for an insight to the life of a lost cousin, and as a picture of what life their ancestral kin experienced in America.

Heritage

Everybody comes from somewhere. Everybody comes from someone. In America today we find a diverse population representing most of the world's cultures, all of its races and many of its ethnic variations. In describing themselves or their heritage we often hear persons say how their forebears came from multiple places. My forbears came from just one place, Denmark. I think I am lucky to be able to say distinctly that I'm Danish and a first-generation American. That both of my parents came from Denmark makes this so. Further, as far as family history has been traced back, their forbears were Danes and lived in Denmark. Identifying with only one ethnic culture helps to retain its traditions as I and my siblings have, in later years, strived to do.

Although our descendants, like most Americans, now have diverse heritages, I would wish for them to know that some of their ancestors came from Denmark and to know of its culture.

It's very little that I know of my parents' life and my ancestors. Grandparents, I knew not at all. My parents may well have shared much with me and my siblings. I may have forgotten much of what they shared. My story of family history is limited to the lives of Niels and Johanne. It begins with all I know of their lives in Denmark.

Niels Mogensen Thordahl
1896-1981

"Niels' Life in Denmark"

Niels was the oldest of seven children and was no doubt expected to take a leadership role early on within the family. He should also expect to inherit what estate that his father had. What was their status in terms of wealth was virtually unknown? What became of that wealth is unknown to me. This is not to suggest there was wealth of any great measure. Regardless, we can presume they resided in a rural environment, although Niels may not have grown up on a farm of any stature. During my first visit to Denmark in 1962, Aunt Jenny took me to the farm where they lived at one time. I sat at the same dinning table at which Far had sat. I signed the guest book. Unfortunately, our lives moved on and I could not identify that farm today.

Life was likely difficult for Niels and his five younger siblings as his mother died before he was ten years old and his father died before he was eighteen years old. The children were lucky to have retained close contact with each other. The youngest child, Jensenius Jacob, (Uncle Jim) was not in contact with the others until Niels learned of his whereabouts. It was sometime after their father died. Niels interceded to prevent Uncle Jim's further separation from the family. His successful intercession to maintain this family unity was regarded by the Thordahl family with certain pride, then as it is today.

Niels Thordahl's Childhood Family
Jensenius (Jim), Asta, Lilly, Jenny, Mette Marie, Niels, Laust

Niels was a great storyteller. One of his most revealing stories was about a childhood incident. As a young lad, maybe fourteen years old, Niels was dispatched by horse and wagon to town with meat to be sold on market day. It seems as though he fell prey to some shysters much as Pinocchio was lured with a promise of gold. These shysters got Niels into a game of cards where the odds were against an amateur gambler. Besides, what did he have for an ante except the meat intended for the butcher? Once that was sold, the action could commence. Things went along fine for a while. Just about the time Niels thought he had this card game mastered his luck changed. Soon all the profit from the sale of his cargo was gone. If meat could be turned into a gambler's stake, then how about the horse and wagon? It was not long before the wagon was also gone. If the horse was to go as well, it would be a long walk home and even greater consequences when he got home. At this point Niels came to his senses and set off for home on the horse. If his father was like his son was to become, when Niels got home there was "hell to pay."

One could easily speculate how this incident may have influenced the rest of his life. Niels would become a master at many card games, especially pinochle. He never liked poker. Part of his business was playing cards in the same sense that playing golf is considered essential to cultivating business associations today. Farming was not to be his forte; like his father, dealing with horses and cattle was.

Perhaps his Viking sense of daring and adventure were also waiting to escape. Niels traveled throughout Denmark and could recall many people and places in those travels.

Two stories stay with me. In our childhood home were two pictures, one was a photograph of "KONG CHRISTIAN RIDER OVER DEN SØNDERJYDSKE GRÆNSE DEN 10. JULI 1920." This was on the occasion of Denmark reclaiming from Germany after WWI the provinces that by plebiscite had voted to be returned to their fatherland. Far had told us that he was among the spectators on hand to witness this historic occasion. Fewer than 100 persons are distinguishable in the photograph. We often scanned this picture attempting to find Far in the crowd. We relied upon identification of his familiar hat, a gray tweed tam. I do not know whether he wore a hat like that in 1920. Far never conceded that we had correctly identified him in the photo. Apparently this photograph was a very popular and prized possession throughout Denmark. I found a surprising mention of it and an explanation of the historical significance for this event in Niels Aage Skov's autobiography, *Letter to my Descendants.*

The second picture was an oil painting of Rebild Park by Jacobsen. This story has a sad ending. Rebild Park is the place in Denmark where each year America's Independence Day is celebrated, the largest such celebration outside America. The rolling hills of purple heather are pictured with a zigzag path leading to a typical low house with a thatched roof, a single chimney on its ridge and a flag on a pole alongside the house. The picture noted that it is a scene of Rebild Park. Niels said he knew the owner of the house, whom we took to be the park's caretakers. Rebild Park is not far from Hald where Niels was born so he could have met this owner. There are a couple possibilities for the real owner. It could have been a picture of Top Hus, which sat on the high point of Rebild Hills at the time, has been restored, and is a focal point in the park now. Another is the "Eagle's Nest" a retreat that was built by Max Renius, a famous Danish chemist who lived in Chicago and became a big supporter of Rebild Park.

Here is my sad story of this painting: This painting has a companion which we always considered of lessor value since it pictures a nondescript pastoral scene. Nowadays I like to think of it as Thor's Valley. Both the pictures were of equal size, large, about 20 by 30 inches, and framed in antique gold leaf. They were a handsome couple on the wall in our formal living room in the post fire house. I do not remember if they were salvaged from the house that burned or were part of the treasures which Far and Ma brought back from their only joint trip to their homeland in 1951.

These pictures came to Bonnie and me as wedding gifts, Far being so thankful that Bonnie had snared me. We attempted to display them in the houses where we lived. However, some houses were too small for proper display. Such was the case of our house on Forbes Air Force Base in Topeka, Kansas. Unfortunately, while we puzzled over where to hang the Rebild Park painting, we left it against the bedroom wall. I believe it was a floor lamp that tipped over, the top slicing a neat gash straight down along one side of the canvas, a few inches from the edge. As I visualize it now, it was not a gapping hole. However, at the time of this tragic accident I was so upset, I immediately removed the canvas and threw out this unique treasure as slightly damaged as it may have been. Not long after, Far visited us and inquired as to the painting, pronouncing that it was now worth 10,000 dollars. Without confessing to its destruction, I managed to assure him that I understood. Thirty five years later, at the urging of Bonnie, I installed a glass mirror into the frame I had saved for so long. Although it has not aged well, needless to say, we are far more cautious of our remaining treasured painting.

Most young boys are curious as to whether their father was ever a soldier. Of course, for Niels this would have been in the Danish army. Danish history or policies at the time of his youth would affect the answer to this question. Denmark was a peaceful, neutral nation at that time. Niels was not inclined to a military character of discipline and obedience. He was more a free spirit who wished to have his say without having to answer to such authority. Barring justification or other means, Niels was required to serve some military duty. According to his army story, he had adequate resources to buy his release from duty after minimal service. Beyond that he also told how the brass buttons on the army uniforms must always be polished. Niels did not prize this task and regularly paid another soldier to polish his brass buttons. He was not allowed a lot of cash on hand, but managed to hide a necessary reserve amount in the barracks rafters.

Once relieved of military duty Niels became somewhat of a soldier of fortune. His story of this adventure was a bit couched. For what must have been significant financial reward he guided others across the border from Germany. It is not clear to me, who these escapees were or why they had to be smuggled out of Germany. Perhaps they were deserters from the Kaiser's army or war service dodgers. Regardless, who knows but this is how Niels earned enough money to travel to America, one last Viking on an expedition of adventure to the New World. Until then his travels had taken him only so far as Germany where he would go to play cards.

JBT 6/2005

Johanne Bjørn
1899-1964

"Johanne's Life in Denmark"

As much as Ma shared Danish life and customs with me, my memory of her self reflection is very limited. Johanne too, grew up on a farm. Perhaps at this time it was the goal of many Danish farmers to elevate themselves from tenant farming to individual ownership. Frequent exchanging and purchasing of farms are evident from the genealogical data of the Bjørn family. During my 1962 visit to Denmark, I visited one of those farms with Aunt Laura and her daughter, Agnethe. In the lower reaches of a field was the site of a water pump and well that Johanne was responsible for keeping in working order. It seemed to be a trying task as this new gadget of the latest technology required careful attention. After fifty years we were able to find the well.

Me, Uncle Niels Pedersen, Laurits, Aunt Laura.

As with American farm life, Danish farm life at the turn of the century was undoubtedly fraught with hardship. Success was not so automatic as it would seem from viewing Denmark's agrarian prosperity today. Today, it would not be a stretch to view Denmark as a breadbasket of poultry and pork. For many Danes their lifestyle and livelihoods are associated with these products and those from the sea.

Although she was accustomed to hardship, Johanne's early years were pierced by unimaginable tragedy. When she was only nine years old, her mother died. As the oldest child, it fell upon Johanne to assume the household chores, including cooking, cleaning and tending to younger siblings. From this early hardship, she learned the hard work that was to become her hallmark. My enduring image of her, which I probably share with my siblings, is of her scrubbing the kitchen floor late at night, when it was bedtime and there was no need for anyone to tread across the dampened hardwood floor.

Beyond her lasting memory of this tragedy, Johanne told of how her father, Niels, went out into his field and chose a common rock as a headstone for his wife's grave. This symbolic act of personal devotion to his lovely Ane is treasured today by their grandchildren as it was by their children. Later, the relocation of this simple stone and its supersession by the marble marker for her stepmother caused some consternation. His love for Ane was further expressed when he gave her name to his first child with Johanne's stepmother.

As difficult as the circumstances were then, within a few months they would become worse. Taking care of the large household was too great a task for a girl who was only ten years old. It was understood and common to society at the time that a housekeeper would be employed in such circumstances. It is also understandable that her father would find another mate. It was common that the housekeeper of necessity would become the mate. So it was for Johanne to have a stepmother. Unfortunately her chores were virtually undiminished and she experienced in her teenage years parental conflict with her stepmother, trouble in a classic sense, a sense worthy of a Hans Christian Andersen dark fairytale.

How did she rid herself of these circumstances? It was something in the nature of being indentured to another farm, perhaps a manor house. Here, work would be much the same, house labor, and it would be her lifelong burden. Except that Johanne spoke fondly of her relationship with her siblings, especially Aunt Laura, we know so little else of her early life. Likely, she sought happiness in the simple things in life, the joy of new life as it entered their house in stepbrothers and stepsisters and participation in Danish customs on holidays. Did she have an active social life or any social life at all? After all, Johanne was nearly thirty years old when she met Niels. She probably had a religious and religiously acceptable life, for later, in America, Johanne seemed to gain strength through her Christian devotion, expressed in the Lutheran church in Gowanda, New York.

I most endearingly think of Ma as a mail order bride. Niels returned to Denmark for what was intended as a short visit. Back from his adventure in America and maybe after some thirty plus years he was ready to settle down. I do not think that he was just looking for a bride. I do think that to him only a Danish girl would do. Regardless, as Ma has told it to me and perhaps other siblings, she was working as a hostess or server at a wedding, one of the few social occasions that were celebrated regardless of a financial shortfall. Niels was in attendance at the wedding. Niels may not have been a formal guest, so he was likely hanging out with the help. They met on this one occasion, exchanged personal contact information, and went on their separate ways. Niels left Denmark, this time for emigration to Canada.

Correspondence by mail became an exchange of love letters. Johanne treasured these letters all her life. Their correspondence progressed for a long time, possibly for a couple years. Finally, came a proposal: "Come to Canada, leave the homeland behind, be married." Imagine how hard it must have been to accept such a proposal from a man she had met only once, to leave a homeland that she loved, to never again see family and friends. Johanne accepted and set off for Canada, for a new life. Three days after disembarking in Halifax, Nova Scotia, she arrived in Ottawa, and married Niels, the man of her dreams, quite literally.

JBT 6/2005

Upon Investigation

Further investigation yields this story of the Danish-American family that starts with Niels Mogensen Thordahl (B. 1896) and his wife, Johanne Bjørn (B. 1899):

Although it was 1931, when they arrived in America together, Niels had been in America before. It has been difficult to find evidence of his early travels to America and within America. We know only from Niels' telling that he had pursued a livelihood in Chicago, Illinois, Texas, and as a miner in Florida.

He probably visited with his Uncle Jens in Clinton, Iowa. He was in contact with Jens after 1930, although he probably did not see him again prior to Jens' death. Niels' uncle, Jens Nielsen

About 1927

Thordahl, was the first of our Thordahl family known to have emigrated to America. According to data available on genealogy web sites, Jens died on May 11, 1932, (listed as Thorndahl) and is buried in Springdale Cemetery in Clinton, Iowa. County records include an Index of Wills, where Jens is listed on page 126 of book 10 (Jens W.). It is accepted that Jens was never married and he had no offspring. The Thordahl name appears a few times in early American records. However, Niels is believed to be the only progenitor of any Thordahl descendants from his family roots, who are now in America.

Johanne Bjørn also had relatives who came to America a generation or two ahead of her. These Bjørns were established in Iowa initially and have since prospered, and their descendants are now located in several places in America. During her life in America, Johanne had nominal contact with the Bjørns of Iowa. There is only one known in-person contact between them, when Niels and Johanne, after their eight children were grown, visited with them in the late 1950s. Years later Bjørn family reunions have brought the descendants of the Bjørn families in America and the Bjørn families in Denmark together periodically.

The Bjørn Family reunions were started through the efforts of cousins, Hanne Bjørn and Eivind Lillehoj from Iowa, during his teaching assignment in Denmark. Hanne is a genealogist and the keeper of the Bjørn family tree records and many other family trees. She has also identified the location of the Thordahl ancestral farm. One of the Bjørn family ancestral farms, Bjørnegaarden, was retired recently after being under Bjørn stewardship for three centuries. One ancestor of the Bjørn family is traced to the earliest legal records in Denmark. Hanne Bjørn maintains the Bjørn family tree back to Johanne's grandfather and grandmother, who had six children, the youngest being Niels. Johanne is the only progenitor of Niels Bjørn's descendants who are now in America.

A bit of Niels' story can be found in a Thordahl Family Record which is written in Danish and in the possession of some family members in Denmark. In regards to Niels' family, here is what it says, as, in an academic exercise using only dictionaries, I have translated it from the Danish words:

I. A. 1. <u>Niels Mogensen Thordahl</u>, horse and cattle dealer, was born in Hald, on the 14th of October 1896 and was married in Canada on the 19th of March 1930 to <u>Johanne Bjørn</u>, who was born in Orum Sdrl. on the 26th of November 1899 and died in USA on the 27th of April 1964. She was the daughter of a farmer, Niels Bjørn and his wife Ane Andreasen, from Orum Sdrl.

Niels Mogensen Thordahl did school in Vejaard and at a young age went to USA, where he still lives and is a retired farmer. In USA. he worked at many different things besides farming. He has been a butcher, a horse and cattle dealer. He has been a mine worker in Canada and in a different way in Florida. He has now been living in the same place for more than 25 years at Buffalo, N. Y. He has traveled around a good deal and been home here (to Denmark) 3 times.

Johanne Bjørn was a housekeeper in Haarby, before she came to Canada in March 1930 and was married. Johanne Bjørn's ashes are buried in Orum Sdrl.

Their Children: a. Carl Bjorn Thordahl
b. Ann Bjorn Thordahl
c. William George Bjorn Thordahl
d. Katherine Joan Bjorn Thordahl
e. Lorne Bjorn Thordahl
f. Niels Arne Eugene Bjorn Thordahl
g. James Bjorn Thordahl
h. Edna Mary Bjorn Thordahl

(The children's Bjørn name is now spelled with the English alphabet. The retention of ancestral names is a proud tradition in the Danish culture.)

The Thordahl Family record also continues as follows:

Niels Mogensen Thordahl was home in 1951 and wrote the following to leave a memory to Kaergaard:

We are home in Denmark in the summer of 1951 and will try to give our contribution to the memory book here in Simested. It is disappointment nr. 1, and as the oldest of her children whose heading is "Ane," so as to know of the family, we will try to tell about our life derived in America, since our journey (to there). (Use of the Danish word"skuffe" is perhaps not correct here. It means "disappoint" so I have tried to translate it as if Niels was lightly bemoaning his elderliness.)

So it was in the summer of 1924 that Niels Mogensen Thordahl went to Canada and after working on a farm for a while, it was, as they say, off to see the world, the great America and coming all the way down to Florida. I lived there until I returned home to Denmark in the Spring of 1927. I was home for only a short time and traveled back to Canada, where we were married in 1930. We lived first in Toronto, Ontario where shortly our oldest child was born on February 26, 1931, but we moved to the USA, coming to the Buffalo, New York area. We are living on a different farm where I had both a horse and cattle dealership. But eventually it became less good, when horses were not used for work anymore and livestock were a good deal expensive. In 1942 we bought a farm and there the eight children were raised. All the children have taken part in looking after the farm and they are who do so but we now are home. We ourselves are pleased to come back to them with all these happy memories that we have received by renewal from childhood and younger days, and to tell them all about the goodness that we have seen in Denmark, about all the warm and sincere welcome we have received everywhere. We say a heartfelt thank-you for the feeling it gave us and also that we belong home here in the family.

In some of the translation I could hear Far talking and feel the emotion that I know they experienced, when Niels and Johanne were lucky to have made a visit of several months, home to Denmark, after twenty years in America, where they had left behind eight children, age nine to nineteen. Upon returning to their children, they confided how, when they first arrived in Denmark and were greeted by their families, they could not recall their Danish and could only shed tears.

As Niels related above, after returning to Denmark for a visit, he emigrated to Canada. I have researched Canadian immigration records and ships' lists and did not find any data regarding his trips to the Americas. We know from Johanne's telling that they met during this sojourn and, after his return to Canada, they corresponded by mail. We cannot determine how long this correspondence took to evolve into a relationship that led to Johanne coming to Canada for marriage. We can trace Johanne's arrival at Halifax, Nova Scotia on the Scandinavian America Lines ship, the Frederick VIII, on March 16, 1930. Johanne proceeded immediately to Ottawa where the adventurous couple were married on March 19.

It might be fun to speculate as to what prior arrangements for these nuptials Niels had made. What type of ceremony was performed? By whom was a ceremony performed? Who were the witnesses or were there any? Niels was a gregarious young man who had made acquaintance with many fellow immigrants in Canada, although his friends may not have lived near Ottawa. It is most likely Niels was living in or near Toronto, Canada, and most of his friends were fellow Danish immigrants. It seems that they had some celebration of the union at which these friends were guests. Printed cards that were customary for these occasions at the time indicate they had a party or reception. You might think of them as a wedding invitation packet where RSVP cards are included.

Now comes a period of less knowledge about the days of the young family. There are several questions for which we need answers:

Why did they move from Canada to the States, to America? Perhaps after his earlier expedition, seeing America as so many did, as "the land of opportunity," it became his goal. Was Niels' first trip to America more than excursion for adventure? Was it the first step in an escape from an unhappy or unfruitful prior period? A direct inquiry to the family in Denmark conveyed that they have concluded that Niels left Denmark to find a "new life." One might also infer from his brief return visit to Denmark in 1927 that he was convinced that his best opportunity resided in the land across the Atlantic.

From Alien registration data, it also appears that, although they were established in Canada, Niels had decided to move to America and had come ahead early to prepare for the move. Niels entered the United States at Niagara Falls on September 27, 1930, and Johanne first came through the same entry point on November 9, 1930. The young couple with their first child, Carl, made the permanent move to America on April 8, 1931. What a wonderful thought that, in the midst of the Great Depression, they still saw such promise in the land that Niels recalled in 1951 as "the great America." Their spirit of adventure was emboldened by a sense of self confidence, an assertion that would carry them through life.

Did they know anyone in America? We know that they came to Buffalo, New York and lived in a small cottage at the home of George and Katherine Zeufle. In 1930 the Zeufle family lived at 89 Andover Street. Katherine came from Canada in 1896. Perhaps Niels and Johanne had met some of her family in Canada. According to census data, George was the assistant treasurer for a coal company. Could this have been another contact that Niels had made when he had earlier worked in mining in Canada?

How long did the young family live in Buffalo? It is probable that they lived there until Ann, their second child, was born, as she is their only child who was born in a Buffalo hospital. What occupation did Niels first pursue in Buffalo? We know that at sometime during the depression he operated a milk delivery business. Then came the infamous realization that his forte was for the same business he had first known. It was the same as his father's business in Denmark, dealing in horses and cattle. It was a business that Niels would know and grow for more than twenty years from a location near Angola, New York, subsequently, to a farm in the township of North Collins, New York.

The Alien registration data, which we know, might raise questions about Niels' first visit to America. Did he not register then or was he not required to register? Did his registration lapse? Did this require him to get a new Alien Registration number? Niels and Johanne never became American citizens. Every January they went to the United States Post Office and registered again as aliens. Niels once related that he returned to the Immigration Service office to apply for citizenship. He was met by an officious, arrogant bureaucrat, a clerk no less, who treated him in a degrading manner, whereupon he vowed to never return. He stubbornly kept that vow.

A Difficult Start

The Great Depression of the nineteen thirties subdued the lives of most American families. Amid the struggle of this period young children could be largely unaware of their hardship. Because their neighbors and friends were in much of the same situation, to them, it was normal. This was undoubtably the case for Niels and Johanne's young family. However, upon later reflection such highlights as getting a new dress for a school pageant could be a poignant memory. They depended on hand-me-down clothing that initially was donated to their family by understanding friends and neighbors. This practice was routine in those difficult days and lasted throughout the early years for all their children. For their home, Niels usually bought second-hand furniture from auctions, although furniture too sometimes came from the generosity of friends. It was not a time for anything to be bought new, except shoes. Before school began in September, Niels took the children en mass for new shoes and as usual negotiated a bulk buy discount.

Caring for an ever growing family meant sharing the household tasks, with older children tending to the younger siblings and helping with cleaning and baking. Wood stoves were the standards at this time and baking up to five loafs of bread three times a week was necessary to feed the family. At one point a satisfactory stove was not available and after the bread had raised the children would pull a wagon loaded with the oven ready bread to a neighbor's farm to be baked. Bread slices were toasted in the oven, yielding a homemade bread treasure that just cannot be equaled in an electric toaster. Delicious pancakes, referred to as *"panny cakes,"* possibly a child's word infused by Niels and Johanne's native language (*pandekager*), were prepared in a large skillet. Being more like crepes, they were filled with jelly, rolled, and eaten with our hands.

The whole family would take part in other tasks. These included canning and butchering animals. Even the youngest child could help. Pealing and slicing peaches and tomatoes and snapping beans for a year's worth of canned food required many hands. Plucking chickens for the Sunday roast was a frequent job. Geese were the fare for Christmas and Thanksgiving only.

Sometime in the mid thirties Niels moved the young family to the country, first to Lockport, then to the rural plain south of Buffalo, New York. Here the land sloped gently up from the shore of Lake Erie. Here were small towns and small family farms, primarily dairy farms. The topography is similar to north-central Jutland, similar to the homeland and, except for the hot summers, the climate was similar too. This would be a good new place to call home.

Niels rented a farm from the bank, a farm in mortgage foreclosure, the Fuller farm. It was the middle of the Great Depression. Farms in mortgage default were taken by the banks and then rented by the banks at reasonable prices until the banks found buyers. A new owner was found for the Fuller farm and the family moved down the road to the Newman place under the same bank rental arrangements. Niels struggled to make a livelihood out of farms owned by the bank. By now he had a small truck, just large enough for one cow.

One day Niels bought a young heifer. He made a couple more stops on his way home with the animal still in the truck. At one farm he received an unsolicited offer for the calf. Not intending to sell his new heifer, he countered with a price that would turn a handsome profit. Surprised at an acceptance he was obligated to complete the deal. Niels arrived home and having made such good profit for the heifer announced that he was done working and henceforth he would be a trader, a horse and cattle dealer, like his father had been. Johanne was not too taken with the idea, being such a spur of the moment decision as it was. That is the way it would be though! From then on Niels oft repeated that he would sell anything he had, if by doing so, he turned a profit. We saved any metal trash we had and periodically Far would haul a load of metal to Buffalo and sold it at the scrap yard. We would disassemble, bolt by bolt, large broken farm machinery and add it to the load to make the trip worthwhile.

Business went along well for a few years. Children were born regularly, so that by 1942 the family numbered a healthy ten. The world was at war again and the economy was recovering. Although gasoline was rationed, Niels always had extra gas coupons which he shared with his friends in Buffalo, an act of kindness that was never forgotten. The bank found a buyer for the Newman place and it was time to move again. This time Niels made a big decision and a bigger move. About ten miles away in the town of North Collins, along U. S. Highway 62, he came across a farm that was held in an estate. By an agreement with the executor, for a payment of 25 dollars a month, Niels bought the place in 1942 for 3200 dollars. He owned this farm, about a hundred acres, until he was retired.

There was a large house on one side of the highway and a little-used barn on the other. Both sides of the barn were painted with an advertisement to "Chew Mail Pouch Tobacco Treat Yourself to The Best." It kept the barn painted for no cost, a shrewd deal and example of Niels' frugality. Later an oil company paid to have their sign on the property. It was a common advertising concept at the time. The neighbor's farm had the famous series of catchy signs of an irrelevant slogan ending simply with "BurmaShave."

Beyond having the tobacco advertisement on the barn the most significant feature of the farm was the swamp.

"The Swamp"

Erosion over thousands of years had reduced the hills that the Ice Age had rolled up in Northeast America and filled the corresponding gorges with soft silt. Now, as the water collected in the shallow valley and struggled to find an outlet, it welcomed a new ecosystem—a swamp. The swamp seemed to start at one edge of our farm and end at the other. It was truly our swamp. Our swamp was dissected by the Erie-Lackawanna railroad as the tracks crossed our land at a right angle, severing the lower forty from the rest of the farm. To the railroad men this stretch was known as The Big Mud Hole, a troublesome span. To us it was a grand area of challenge and adventure.

The swamp consumed almost half of the lower forty and the remainder had poor soil and a few acres of forest. The swamp trees were crippled by perpetual submersion and simply stood in lifeless acknowledgment. We could get to that section of the farm by a very steep grade for horse and wagon, the same as the adjacent farms, although their crossing grades were suitable for tractors and even motor vehicles. There was little call to cross the tracks.

On the opposite side of the tracks, the near side, the swamp consumed several acres, making a more traditional bog with plants that thrived in this steamy environment, cattails and water lilies. We often explored the wonder of our swamp from the tracks, first putting our ear to the rails to sense if a train was coming. Only a few times did we find ourselves dashing for the bushes along the track bed. More often we hustled back to the gate or were sitting on our gate waiting and hailing to the engineer and the men in the caboose as the trains passed. It was in the day of steam engine driven trains with their coal-stoked exhaust puffing out from a big funnel on top the engine, a classic picture of the times.

From our perch we tried to follow the path of the souvenirs as they sailed from the rails when the iron wheels smashed the pennies that we had placed on the rails. Only once were we successful when a single new diesel engine crept along with men riding outside on its front end. We sat in silent fear that our federal offense would be exposed and hoped that the usual wave to the railroad inspection crew would distract them from their task. This time the pennies plopped quietly from the rails and we finally had our illegally destroyed coins.

Wildlife was the main attraction of the swamp. It was the only home in the area to muskrats with their intriguing mounds of cattail stalks for homes. We kept track of their mounds to know how well these harmless creatures were faring in their swamp haven. Family huts numbering only seven seemed to be enough to call it a thriving colony. Once I found a muskrat on the railroad tracks, killed by a speeding train. Live muskrats remained unseen. I mentioned my find to Walter Tomaszewski at school. He thought he could get five dollars for the muskrat pelt. I had no idea muskrats were of any value for their fur. I agreed to bring the dead animal to school the next day and he would forgo the school bus so he could carry it home on his bicycle, a treacherous ride on icy roads. I returned to the kill site and found it undisturbed. However, a closer examination showed that the carcass had not been adequately preserved on the heat absorbent track bed.

Another time, an enigmatic creature appeared in the muddy water of a pool where the swamp water sought to escape under the railroad tracks. We could take this shortcut too, when the dry season had lowered the water level and gave some hope that greater farmland might be gained. This year the drought left only a tiny pool under the railroad. The haven for snapping turtles had turned to mud. We marked our way across the cracked mud stepping stones to this last water hole. Something moved below the dark surface. We could not determine what it was and dubbed the creature, Four Whiskers. Occasionally it surfaced, still indistinguishable, with just its whiskers revealed in the muddy pond. We tried, unsuccessfully, to catch the slimy beast.

I deferred, choosing to treasure the creature from the swamp as a mystery deserving to haunt our imagination.

Then one day my little sister, Edna, snuck down to the swamp. Up through the dry grass she returned, carrying the puzzle on a piece of bark, repeatedly shouting triumphantly long before she could be heard from the house, "I caught Four Whiskers. I caught Four Whiskers." At that moment I hated her. If Four Whiskers was to be caught, if the mystery was to be solved, why did it have to be solved by her? Why did it have to be a girl who solved it, capturing a pitiful catfish?

It was a marginal farm with a small plot on the hillside and an even smaller parcel across Wilcox Road. The main portion of the farm, about a hundred acres, was west of the highway where the hill gave way to arable fields that sloped gently down to the bottomland—the swamp. Far thought, if he cut a trench through the swamp, it would help to drain it. Hitching a hand plow behind a team of horses he drove them through a likely drainage route. The huge water lily roots, thick as a man's arm, ripped the plow from his hands and ended that endeavor. The swamp would remain.

After thousands of years in the making, it is more robust than ever. On last observation, more than fifty years since those days of exploring nature, I noted that our swamp, my treasure island, surprisingly, has doubled in size.

JBT 11/2006

Our old barn in its last days with swamp to the far right.

A Butcher Too

Niels often butchered a calf and rarely a sheep or pig. None of the animal was wasted. Soap would be made from the tallow and meat from the animal's head was made into headcheese. Even the brains were eaten. Butchering sheep was not a favorite of Niels. Mutton is fairly strong meat on the best of days. Far said, "If the wool from the sheep touched the skinned meat, it would impart a further disagreeable strongness to the meat." I go with what he said about turkeys too, "If you want a true turkey taste you need a tom turkey." Even for a small family Thanksgiving dinner I always bought a turkey that weighed at least twenty pounds, a tom.

When it comes to selecting good meat, I think Far knew what he was talking about. After all, he had been a butcher too. We butchered a pig one time. To clean the pig, we scalded it in a huge iron kettle. This made it easier to scrape its bristles off. The work needed to heat a huge kettle of water over an open fire meant we did not butcher a pig very often.

Goats, however, were the meat of choice, until it was time to kill a horse. We anticipated that task with awe and wonder. How could we manage this huge task? In what manner could we subdue such a big animal? To store so much meat, a bin was rented in a walk-in freezer at the grocery store in Eden, a village on the way to Buffalo, a route taken almost weekly in Far's business.

"Killing Horses"

(With apologies to equine fans)

Years ago before I "retired" I rode in a van pool some many miles to work. It was the van driver's misfortune to own a couple of riding horses and to tell often of his adventures and misadventures with his sometimes untrusty steeds. Finally, I thought to share my experiences, knowledge and fondness for horses or to be more precise horse meat. So, I asked Dan, the van pool driver, if he knew how to kill a horse. I was well rewarded with his expression of astonishment when I described in gruesome detail how Far with the help of his sons butchered the stately beast.

"A horse is a horse of course." With that in mind think not of his handsome stance, his satin sheen, his haughty gait as he parades to the post with a rider in saddle to compete in the sport of kings. Think not of his sinuous shoulders collared with harness, his hefty haunches heaving as he hauls the farmer's load of hay. Rather think of the family of ten sharing a small farm in Western New York with chickens and geese, a cow or two and, foods so few. Think of the treat it would be when the day arrived that we all would eat steak, horsemeat steak. Though it was rare, maybe but once a year, the time had come to savor this feast.

By what criteria the animal to be sacrificed was selected I do not know. Perhaps he was too old or too young to work or never trained for harness. Was the likely tenderness of its meat a factor? At the time none of this was of much concern to me. What I was interested in was the deed. First the barn must be made ready. Just inside the double sliding doors was a floor of heavy planks, polished with wear and easy to sweep clean. From the beams for the hay loft we attached a strong pipe and fixed it with a block and tackle. From this pipe the carcass would be hung.

Niels often blindfolded a horse to load it onto the truck or bring one into a strange stable. This time the horse was blindfolded for different reasons. He should not duck. He should not be shy. He should not be fearful and try to run. The horse is captured by halter and leader. Across his eyes and secured under the halter straps Far has placed a burlap bag. It must not cover the horse's forehead for that is a vital spot, a target that must be steady and clear.

The deed is done in a flash. Holding the horse's leader in left hand and facing the horse eye to blindfold, with one swing of an axe, its flat head being used like a hammer, Far smacks the horse, hitting the target with surprisingly little force. (You might say, "He never knew what hit him.") Stunned, the victim drops to his front knees with a heavy thud, frozen stiff and erect. Clearly exposed just beneath the skin on his breast is the next target, the horse's heart. With one thrust of a sharp dagger Far administered the final blow. Blood flows quickly and smoothly straight from the heart. As Far gathers the blood in a bucket we quickly snare the horse by the ankles of its hind legs and begin to hoist it by the tackle. Once the guts are withdrawn, the task is much easier and butchering the animal becomes more routine.

Though I may have described this gory tale quite vividly, what I remember best is steak that evening, all you could eat horsemeat steak, fried by Far—the only time he ever stood at a stove or served food while Ma was alive.

JBT 9/2004

Fun on the Farm

We did many exciting things for fun (ha), like building jigsaw puzzles and playing cards. We were so familiar with some puzzles, having built them so many times, that we timed how fast we could build them. The best puzzles at that time had really thick pieces, at least a quarter inch thick. Niels did not participate when the kids were building puzzles, although he may have pieced together picture puzzles for his personal relaxation. Before we were school-age, Edna and I had ridden on one of his trips to Buffalo. We were tantalized by a package that Far had placed in the truck when we started our return trip. We were sure it was a gift for us, a surprise that Far would not reveal in spite of our pleas. We were really surprised and disappointed to learn when we got home that the package contained two jigsaw puzzles that were not for us.

It seems that we always knew how to play pinocle. We learned simply by watching the card game when Far played with his good friends. We had only one board game which I remember, Monopoly. We did have an Ouija Board that was generally used to traumatize the younger kids. Being next to the youngest, I fell victim to it's "wisdom" more often than I wish to recall. Only recently was I finally convinced that Ouija's power lay in the hands of a mischievous sibling.

Outdoor recreation was more pleasing. It was easy to put together a bunch of kids to play Hide and Seek. Sneaking "home free" was our goal, although there was always one or two who remained hidden until the rest lost interest in further play. My favorite was Kick the Can. The game began with a strong kick to an old can. While the person who was "It" retrieved the can; we hid. "It" looked for the others and raced them to the can when

"It" found each one. If you could beat "It" to the can and kick the can again, a new round was started.

Their eight children and Uncle Jim

We had a teeter-totter like none other. We all had bicycles which we often painted and repainted with "v" shaped designs on the tail of the fender. My first bicycle, I bought from the neighbor when I was about thirteen. I paid fifteen dollars for it. I still have it too. We made our own stilts using Ma's clothesline booster poles. In the hay loft we fashioned a swing that operated like a glider with two ropes suspended from beams to support a sixteen-foot long plank. There was room for all who wanted a ride. When we really got the plank swinging, we could smack the barn walls.

When outside, the barn walls made a great place to play ball by yourself. I made up a game that amounted to baseball by valuing each rebound and tracking the progress of players in some handmade score sheets. My league included a number of teams, my favorite being the Yankees. I had one pinball-like game called Bagatelle which worked like baseball too. The modern electronic versions that I have seen do not hold a candle to it. When we got strong enough to toss a ball over the barn that became a favorite challenge. "Ollie ollie over," we yelled to alert the receiver on the other side of the barn to watch for the ball. Otherwise, for batting practice we used sticks and peppered stones into the field. Of course, we gathered just the right stones. Wearing out good batting sticks also became a problem as the stones regularly took chunks of wood out of these bats.

Ma strongly encouraged our play as she recognized the value of exercise as she recalled from her childhood. She stretched for exercise every morning. One day she joined us in the yard where we were riding our bicycles. She challenged herself to see how well she could still ride a bicycle. Unfortunately, she came too near the steep slope by the milk house and tumbled, uninjured—a little frightened though. Bill was there to help her up. Neither Niels nor Johanne participated in recreational activities with the children. Besides being older than the average parents, it would be two generations before physical play between parents and children was to become popular. Far was generous in taking the children to the swimming hole in the creek by Taylor's Grove, about two miles away. He sat in the truck reading the newspaper until we returned from the creek in the gulch.

With the neighbor kids we played Cowboys and Indians. Each vied for the top role: the Lone Ranger. Then there was the Cisco Kid and Hop-a-Long Cassidy whose horse required a certain gait that added to the fun. Fortunately there was always a need for a side kick like Tonto or Pancho. We did not have guns like the neighbor kids. For a rifle, I used a piece of wood that was shaped a bit like a gun. I was very proud of its likeness to a Winchester 73 with a roll pin for a sight and nail for a trigger.

We made our own fun.

"The Toy Farm Enterprise"

If you asked me, "What was your favorite toy in childhood?"
I would draw a blank. Better I could tell about "the enterprise."
That would go a long way to describe childhood fun on the farm
before the house burned down or about that time. Most of the
playground age Thordahl children took part in this enterprise.

Along the small stream that ran beside the old house is where
it took place. The stream was not much more than a ditch with
a steady trickle of water even at the driest time of the year. In
most places the ditch was not more than three to five feet deep
and seven to eight feet across. On the far side of the ditch was
an old strawberry patch. So there was ample reason to cross the
ditch in addition to taking a shortcut to hike up old Wilcox Road.
We should have a bridge across this ditch where the footpath led
to where a slight leap would carry you across the water at the
bottom of the ditch. That would be just the beginning.

It was a small bridge that we built about thirty feet up the
stream from where you approached this sanctuary hidden behind
the old corn crib and a large elm tree. From there would grow a
farmland of make-believe. Immediately across the bridge was a
patch of tender grass that always seemed right for cutting. This
patch made great hay fields for stock that would need feed on our
farms. Somehow without dispute we each claimed a space for
miniature agricultural homesteads. Sticks for fenceposts were
strung together with white twine for boundaries. Barns of some
nature were built or maybe a wooden crate would do. On the
near side of the ditch the footpath was converted to a highway.
Along the other side we fashioned proper farm roads.

Finding the necessary toys to be used as farm implements
presented more of a challenge. The "real McCoy" toys in our
world were few. Those who had them were envied without a
word. Some toy tools were made and utensils from Ma's kitchen
could always be put to use. Mostly though, we got our toys

from the dump on Wilcox Road, a site of frequent fascination and anticipation. It was there where I came across my favorite treasure, a truck. Well, it was not a real toy truck. It was just a metal box with wheels. It was outsize for the roads and buildings in our enterprise. However, to me it was the best truck around. With that truck I am sure I was envied by my siblings.

Our enterprise is where we spent time at play, to a degree an effort that approached work. We expanded the enterprise with another bridge just where you entered our sanctuary. This was not just a toy bridge down in the ditch. It spanned the widest point and could easily carry a load of several adults. Laid securely on two old beams were thin strips of hardwood placed diagonally over used boards that formed the walkway. The walkway was further framed by side rails, extending up even with the diagonal slats, so that the bridge was not only strong but appealing to the pedestrian. Early craftsmanship and fledgling engineering wings were being developed and tested. Another bridge was tried in the chasm of barren land further up the stream. Even though it was just a board, big enough for a toy, it further expressed personal endeavor and a spirit of exploration.

Usually we would reenact familiar farm activities from our daily chores or farm work we had seen on the larger, real farms, around our home. We played at trips to the auctions in Springville and Sherman with which we were so familiar that being integral to Far's business of trading livestock. The favorite activities were harvesting hay and planting our fields. The fields were tilled with a spoon for a plow and raked with fingers. As the corn grew it was cut to prevent it from overwhelming the play size plots of grain. Of course, first you had to turn the hard dirt with a shovel to make a dirt patch suitable for play. We cut the wild grass with the cup of our hand. Just like in the real farm we laid the grass in windrows to dry and be loaded on small wagons by a conveyer, an imaginary hay loader. Then it was off to the barn where hoisting it into the hay loft using fingers for a grappling hook. Most of the play tasks took more than one player to execute. It was a time of unparalleled sibling cooperation.

Surprisingly our enterprise was kept in secret. Perhaps that was simply because we felt it was no great achievement. Who would be interested in it? More likely though, we feared some objection to our waste of effort. A project that appeared to take so much work should be more fruitful. After the house burned, that parcel of land where it stood was to be sold. Niels had already found a buyer.

If we could not stop the sale, we would lose our sanctuary. With understood trepidation and a hint of pride we dared to expose our treasured enterprise to Ma. We politely pleaded for her to stop Far from selling off—"our" land. Ma admired our achievement with silent pride. It was not necessary for her to say a word. We knew the outcome before we had asked. So far as I know, Far was never aware of our toy farm enterprise.

With our farms gone, just as in each challenge in the rest of our lives, we moved on with just a proud memory.

JBT 9/2004

Farm Pets

On a farm there is always room for pets. On our farm some pets were farm animals and some, man's best friend.

Deuce, a Dog

The first pet that I remember being in our household was a big black dog named Deuce. Deuce was probably a mixed breed of shepherd, collie, and other. If you wanted to boast about him, and I am sure the family did, you could say he was gentle, friendly, and tolerated children well, all common ways to describe a good dog today. When we were three and four years old, Far would have us demonstrate how when we jumped on Deuce he would not bite. However, I did learn where not to land. In the end I feared jumping on Deuce more than I feared walking under the belly of a horse, which we did regularly, when Far wanted to demonstrate how gentle was a horse that he was trying to sell. This was one of Far's favorite and most convincing sales pitches. Today, I do not recommend either challenge.

Deuce was a legitimate ranch dog. He needed little encouragement to take after stock with a commanding bark and persuasive nip at their heels to drive stock into the barn. More than once he managed to avoid a nasty hoof kicked in his direction. As reprisal he answered with greater determination. Even when he became too old for this activity, he could not be restrained. In his old age he was afflicted with hind quarter paralysis, a common ailment for large dogs. When one last time he tried hard to chase a horse up the hill behind the barn, propelling himself by front legs only, his rear legs dragging uselessly behind, it was time to put him out of his misery.

That may sound cruel. However, in those days on the farm, that is what you did. Further, veterinarians for us were not in the business of pet care. They were for farm stock. This business was left to the pet's owner. We really did not have the means to end Deuce's life by the consensus method, a gun. A neighbor who owned a rifle was asked to do the deed. To a degree, this lessened the moral crisis caused by killing your own pet. As the executioner approached him, Deuce sought to escape and headed into the weeds beside the barn. With a single shot and a thud it was over. I do not remember who buried him or any afterthoughts, unlike today, (September 14, 2004), when earlier I laid Max, Riley's pet hamster, in a small box for a casket.

And then there were

Geese

In the interlude between Deuce and the next dog, I struck up a relationship with geese. In case you did not know, let me tell you the nature of geese. Geese are perhaps the most uncivil characters on earth. They hang out in a gaggle making a horrendous noise whenever another of any species comes near. If they are unsuccessful in scaring off the intruder with a lot of racket, they flap their wings in a blustery display, a bluff of meanness that is not far below the surface. When that surface erupts, with wings stretched wide and thrusting their necks straight ahead, they attack with sharp beaks. How does anyone manage to claim a friend in geese? They have that one weakness common to all species. They like to be fed. If you feed them from early on in their life, you might have a chance to fracture their mean exterior and come to an understanding, as I did with a small gaggle until they were well grown and decided to take on the nature of their older cousins. It came to where I could no longer pick them up. They never chased me though or seemed rude. That was reward enough from a goose.

There was one goose which had a special place in my heart. I am sure, if he had a heart, there was a special place in it for me. I called him Squeaky. He was lame, having been born with a crippled foot, and often limped off alone only to become lost. He left it to me to find him. There were times he was stymied by an obstacle that presented no challenge to the others. Whatever the situation was, I knew when he was in trouble. "Squeak, squeak, squeak," he would clack to no end, so I could find him. Even when he fell into a hole in the garden, although he knew he should not be there, he squeaked for me. There I found him face down in a hole, just his tail sticking out. If he had not made a frantic, muffled squeak, I could not have rescued him. How could you not love a goose like that? I loved Squeaky as much as any seven-year-old could love a goose.

My greater love, though, was for:

Goats

Kids with kids

Goats always had a special place in my life. On our farm, their lives were usually short. As cute as kids are, we knew to not get too attached to them. Someday they would make a meal that I remember as the very best. Still nothing topped the night Far came home with twins from the auction in Sherman. When he announced there were a couple of kids in the truck, we thought, "How did he get them home in the cattle truck full of bigger animals, horses?" You could not have them ride in the cab, although there was plenty of room for a couple of baby goats. They would be far too mischievous and unsafe to have so near the driver. We had forgotten about the separate compartment over the truck cab that was accessed from a door at the side. To load them up it meant hoisting those cute little critters over your head while standing on the running board. From that time on, I admired Far's resourcefulness.

There was one very special dog:

"My Dog, Nanny"

"Every boy should have a dog," was a popular sentiment years ago, when I was a boy. Nanny would become my dog. I could say "pet." However, on a farm a dog is not just a pet. On our farm a dog must have more value; a dog must work; a dog must at least boss animals. Rounding up or corralling horses and cows like a trained sheep-herding dog might be a bit much to ask. At least our dog should make a cow or horse load onto the truck. If a bark was not enough, a nip to the horse's hock would usually show them who was the boss. Imagining Nanny as the boss is a stretch.

She was just a puppy, a little bundle of fur, when Far brought her home one evening. He had gotten the puppy at the cattle auction, free of course. You do not invest cash in an animal that might "amount to nothing" more than a pet. Did Far have in mind that she could replace Deuce, our former dog? He was a big black dog, an animal-boss dog, a really kid-friendly dog, just the kind of dog a family with eight kids needed. How would such a cute little puppy become such a dog? She was white, a pure white that belied any suggestion of authority. Would she need training? No one in our house had any idea of how to train dogs. What would be her true disposition? We had no way of knowing.

First of course, the new puppy must have a name. She should have a girl name. That pretty much meant I would not have much say in choosing a name. Therefore I cannot remember just how her name was chosen. I believe it came from thoughts about a house helper who was regarded fondly. It may be disrespectful to name a dog after a person. However, if this woman was a child's choice nanny, why not give this puppy a name of love and respect: Nanny?   Oooh, the pain of training a puppy. There was one bit of training that needed no expertise. At least, that is what I was told. Every puppy must be housebroken. You know. They must learn to not use the carpet for a toilet. They must learn to indicate their need to use *their* toilet, the one outside. There was only one known way to perform this training. It meant an act of humiliation and subjugation, an action of determination and resignation. In spite of words of assurance from the older siblings I turned away so as not to see. The first time Nanny piddled on the floor, Ma quickly grabbed her, "rubbed her nose in it," and "threw her out the door." I have to admit; it does the trick. Years later when we should get a puppy for our kids could I perform this trick? Nope! For such a dastardly deed, I would defer to Bonnie.

Nanny largely showed an indifference to me and no real attachment to any member of the family. Until one day, when she was no longer a puppy and not quite a dog of her our nature, that day she grew in my eyes and in my heart. That day she became my dog. Nanny had a bad habit. It was a habit common to many dogs raised in the country, free to roam. They chase cars, trucks and buses, you name it. For some dogs it was sport. For Nanny, if it had wheels, especially a bicycle, it must be chased away. Living on a major highway was frequently fatal for dogs with this habit. We lived on US Highway 62.

Then came that fateful day. Far was in the living room playing cards with the usual cronies. I was just about to go outside when I heard that telltale bark. Nanny was chasing something. Unfortunately, this time it was a boy on a bicycle. This was not a vehicle that warranted a few barks and a half-hearted sprint. This was a vehicle that could be caught. I ran out to stop her. Too late! The mean spirited bike rider had seen an opportunity. He could win this race. It would not take an exhausting dash. Coming along the highway was a truck, a big feed mill truck. As for the rider, I saw his intent; I knew his thought. If he gradually changed his route and steered his bike across the highway, his pursuer would follow this path and right into the path of the truck. Just as I visualized how the accident could happen, it did. What chance for survival did Nanny have?

I ran back into the house, seeking assurance that it was not true. That it would be all right. Interrupting the card game, I stammered, "Far, Nanny got hit by a truck. She's dead . . . in the road." I really was not surprised at his response, "Well, go get a rope and drag her off." I went to do just that. With rope in hand I approached the body. Little white Nanny lay with her head in the right wheel track on the highway. Her body stretched to the side of the road. I could easily tie the rope to a hind leg without going on the pavement. Just as I reached down to secure my recovery line to this beautiful white animal, a dog that had not yet become a pet, she jumped up and ran to the house. There she took refuge under the china cabinet. I did too. As I caressed her and comforted her, a bond grew between a boy and his dog.

Nanny never quite looked the same to me afterward. I felt she never quite saw me the same either. She was not a big dog, smaller than the common shepherd dog, a famous farm worker breed. She never became a good farm-help dog. She never was an overly compromising dog. No one else could really pet her, only me. Yes, Nanny was my dog.

As with the old wive's tale, Nanny would lick a wound on Niels' hand to heal it. For me she licked so many other wounds.

Postscript: Nanny never chased again like before. She did get hit again crossing the road years later. This time she suffered a broken leg. Again she limped to refuge under the china cabinet. I was too big to join her. She knew I was there though. She healed on her own. A Vet for a pet was an expense that would never be considered.

I felt she never got enough to eat. Most every night when we had enough food in the house I would have a bowl of cereal with extra milk, so I could surreptitiously share with her. Otherwise, she got only a few table scraps.

Early on Niels taught Nanny that she was not to eat the hen's eggs she found in the barn. This lesson entailed a mean trick of enticing her with an egg. However, this egg was filled with pepper and mustard powder. Once in its mouth the dog was restrained from rejecting it by manually clamping its mouth shut. If curing a dog with a yen for eggs could not be done successfully in this manner, it was done in.

Nanny had a hate for mice and snakes. I don't know. Maybe all dogs do. She did not eat a rat or mouse that she caught. She would crunch the body in her mouth a few quick times and spit it out. Snakes? She would grab and shake violently until they were dead. Did she have the same aversion to these critters that I do? Nanny was still alive when I left for the Air Force. On my first leave home I could see how she had tired. It was left to Joan to write with the news when Nanny had died and been buried near the garden.

JBT 9/2005

Nanny watches while we husk corn.

Illness in that Era

I do not remember ever going to the doctor, when I was a child. Then again, back in those days, doctors made house calls. I do not remember being sick, although I have come across my second grade report card that indicates I missed more than thirty days of school that year.

I was not without injury though, some treated, some not. It was not a good idea to get hurt, because having to pay for a doctor or emergency first aid was not going to make Far happy. At least, that is how I felt. I chose other alternatives. There was the time I was bending nails over in a useless board just for the fun of it. I stomped on one stubborn nail and missed. The nail went through the side of my shoe and punctured my foot in the soft inner arch. It did not hurt. Just the same, I took my shoe off to check my injury. It was not bleeding. However, a piece of some inner tissue was poking out of the wound. I pushed the worm like membrane back in and quit kicking at nails. Another night just before dark we were playing tag on the wet grass. I slid and smacked my knee, on the inside, on a large boulder left in the yard. My leg went numb; I could not walk. Afraid I would be paralyzed and afraid to tell anyone, I hopped into the house, snuck upstairs and went to bed. Miraculously, the next morning I woke up, able to walk and not even bruised.

As an infant apparently I was not gaining weight as expected. Sister Ann tells me how Ma was always weighing me. This was also a common practice at the time which has since fallen out of use. In its place we make regular visits to baby wellness clinics or pediatricians.

Childhood illnesses that I and the other children suffered were either unrelated to our environment or common, except for Eugene and Bill. Eugene has endured a lifelong battle with asthma. Bill had a bout with rheumatic fever, a disease that, fifty years later, had a devastating effect on heart valves. For those common childhood illnesses, mothering was the best treatment and normally the only treatment we received. Just to have Ma's soft hand hold your forehead when vomiting was satisfactory comfort to ease stomach flu and other ailments. Treatment for sunburn, a common conditioned for us with fair Scandinavian skin, was often debated. Butter for burns, baking powder on blisters, and Vicks Vapor Rub on your chest for colds were principal remedies.

When I was maybe five years old or so I remember Ma being sick in bed and the doctor coming to the house. In those days you were not sick, unless you were "sick in bed." Until she suffered a debilitating stroke, Johanne virtually never saw a doctor. Only the day before, Ma came running, literally, to the car when Bill had stopped at the house for her. With a gentle admonishment Bill questioned, "Ma, will you never slow down?" She was rushed by ambulance to the Tri County Hospital in Gowanda. It was shortly after her sixtieth birthday.

On her birthday, Carl's wife, Anna Jean, and her friend, Jean had stopped in before leaving for a swim at the high school pool. Johanne suggested they have a cup of tea, after all, it was her birthday. Couldn't they just sit for a bit? Instead of going swimming, the three enjoyed a quiet, girls-only celebration, a bit fancier tea than the routine afternoon coffee-break. It was a moment that would never be repeated.

Niels had some sciatica problem for which he had surgery. In the Buffalo hospital Far insisted that he must have beer with his evening meal. Serving beer was absolutely against hospital rules. He convinced the doctor, "Damn the rules." Niels got his beer for dinner. It was not a matter of winning beer; it was a matter of winning the day, having his way.

I skipped school one day to visit Far in the hospital. It was at the invitation of Robert Harkness, a neighbor farmer, who planned to make a neighborly visit and wanted a companion to ride along. Immediately, upon our arrival Far wanted to know why I was not in school. It was near to graduation and all grades were decided, except for final exams and my one incomplete project, that was due that day. I did not say anything about the incomplete project.

Niels' last hospital visit was in the hospital in Gowanda, when non specific illnesses of old age began to befall him. He shared with me his weird dreams which, we later learned, were hallucinations caused be the medicines he was being given without advisement, that he had a right to refuse medications. He asked me to shave his beard. As he pressed his tongue against folds of skin hiding his toothless mouth, I pressed too hard, tilted the blade incorrectly, and nicked his cheek several times with a strange sharp razor. I made a mess of that job and begged to curtail our effort. Later he reached out to me coyly and for the first and only time in my life that I remember, I held his hand. Far was not so ill that he needed hospitalization so Bill and I visited nursing homes where he could stay. I saw him the last time at the nursing home in Springville, a place that was showing its age. Niels stayed there until the new facility in Gowanda was available.

The Old House

I remember growing up in two houses, because the first of these houses burned down. The old house was practical, like most houses were at the time. Houses in western New York's "Appalachia" were not focused on aesthetics. Still, it was a grand house.

It did not have running water per se. Just outside the back kitchen door in the attached wood shed was a toilet. At the far end of the wood shed just before the exit was a hand pump to a well. You could get water from here to flush the toilet. More often than not Johanne used dirty water from the kitchen or laundry. For baths, there was a large galvanized tub placed on the kitchen floor, where, on Saturday night, each child in turn, going from the youngest to the oldest, was bathed in the same water.

From the kitchen you went into the common room, the living room. Here was the only heat, a wood burning pot belly stove midway across the room and away from the windows and well away from the wall on the right as you entered. Behind the stove was a door that led to the stairs. At the top of the stairs was a common room where most of the kids slept. To the right was another bedroom which had two beds in it. From here you could access the attic straight on.

This house, too, was furnished with used furniture that Niels found at auctions or that came from the generosity of neighbors and friends. Modernization of appliances occurred first in the laundry realm. From a wash board we progressed to a wringer washer where the wringer was operated by hand and then to a similar machine where the wringer was power driven. Getting your hand squashed in the rollers was an accepted risk. All the children helped Ma with the laundry when they were old enough. Even the smallest kids could pin socks and small items to the clothesline. Ironing was done by Ma and the other kids, including the boys.

The old house had a nice front yard. Occasionally, a ring of toadstools would appear overnight. Ma told us that the fairies had met there and these were their seats. Straight out from the front of the house beside the road was a stately tree. By the driveway was a small tree in which even a five-year-old boy could climb. I took refuge there one time, when I did not want to go to Sunday school. I was unceremoniously pulled down from the tree and ushered to the car that had come to take us. At the corner of the house was a clump of bushes which had big snowball-like blooms. In the middle of this clump of bushes was a great place to hide or play.

The old house would be home for less than seven years.

The "old" House

"The House Fire"

She was wearing big rubber farm boots and ragged, old, farm pants. I had never seen my mother wear pants. I had never seen my mother cry. She was not crying now. Yet, I could see she was sad, forlorn. As we looked out from the barn, across the street to the blackened remains of our house, I sought to comfort her. "It was an old house," I said. What else could an eight-year-old boy offer now, as words of comfort? Ma replied, "Yes, but, there were a lot of good things in it." It would be many years before I understood what her "good things" were.

Some remember it as the coldest winter day on record in Western New York. I remember gathering in the large living room. It was not the largest room in the house. One large room upstairs was an open bay, a dormitory like room where most of the eight kids slept. With a pot belly stove fired with wood, the living room was the only room that provided a heated space. The stove was offset from the center of the room near to an inner wall. Behind the stove, were the stairs which were closed off by a door. The darkened stairway was a favorite place for me to play and to let my imagination run. This night I found it too cold for a long stay. I joined the others in the living room. The stove was blazing, putting out abundant heat.

Suddenly, we heard loud, sharp, banging noises coming from the attic. We were all puzzled, but oddly, not frightened. This house was a sanctuary in which we always felt safe. We did not hesitate to investigate the cause of the strange noises. First up the stairs was Ma, followed by Bill, the third oldest child. I squeezed as tight as I could behind these leaders within our household. We could enter the attic straight on ducking only slightly through a large door. It was also easy to stand erect in the attic. We never made it that far. I did not get quite close enough to see into the attic.

Later Ma described what she had seen and her thoughts. The stove pipe was red hot and bulging, burping, trying to relieve itself. This was in a horizontal section of stovepipe that carried the fire's exhaust across the attic to the chimney, a span of possibly eight feet. Here was a fatal flaw in design. Perhaps it was the result of modifications to move the pot belly stove to a less obtrusive location. There was a roll of old carpet on the attic floor. Ma gave a thought to tossing this ragged rug over the stovepipe. Then she realized there was no chance. It was time to save the family and what we could save of our necessities, clothes, and family records. I have always measured Ma's strength of character with this vision. Reacting to a crisis, she was superhuman, able to toss a heavy roll of carpet to shoulder height.

The fire company was called with the old party line phone. Could this call summon a miracle? Every hamlet had its Volunteer Fire company which was staffed from their homes by farmers and other men in the neighborhood. The nearest station was in the town of Lawtons, just over a mile away. Surprisingly, the fire truck and its crew arrived within minutes. There was Ernie, Robert and his dad George, and Harold and his dad Adolph. There were others. Our house might be saved after all. Hoses were strung across the highway past the barn to an open well, frozen with inches of ice. Some remember that the fire truck's pumps froze. I remember seeing the first burst of water crash onto the roof, collapsing it and giving a vent to all the oxygen needed to turn the whole house into an inferno. It was not just water that caused the roof to cave. Within a second the pumper was blasting mud from the bottom of the well and all hope was lost. With no other resources available, the fire raged until nothing but a cellar full of ash remained.

Still there were some small victories, small miracles. Days later we sifted through the basement of ash. We found a few silver coins that had dropped down from Far and Ma's bedroom. We found a five-gallon can of peanut butter. Although a charred taste remained after peeling away the ash and singed crust, we delighted in claiming a small victory by eating sandwiches made from its contents. To my everlasting amazement, these inexperienced farmer firemen had salvaged, from the flames, a dresser full of our clothes. Consider this! That dresser was located upstairs and retrieved unscathed in the dark. My heroes.

For a few months we had a home in the upper apartment of a generous neighbor's huge farmhouse. In the summer a new house would be built across the street with such modern conveniences as indoor plumbing, a furnace in the basement, a fireplace, and five bedrooms.

"A lot of good things" had a new home. That day in the winter of 1949 was the only time I ever saw Ma wear pants.

Postscript: To this day, when I see a stovepipe I assess, in my mind, its verticality and the risk it poses to cause a fire like the one that destroyed our "Old House."
JBT 10/2005

The New House

The "new" house which we built across the street was also practical, more open, and after some improvements it was quite aesthetic. I say "we built" because everyone played a part in its construction. Each could best measure their contribution. I remember painting, lead base enamel paint, I'm for sure, because it was difficult to clean the paint brushes. Then, on the inside, there was the drywall to nail, tape and fill. The skill tasks, such as masonry and cutting the timber in our forest and processing it at the saw mill, were done by Niels' friends, as a favor or to relieve a debt which they owed to Far.

Fred Damerau, the bricklayer, came with a crew that he normally worked with and laid the basement block walls in a single day. Niels had lent money to a sawmill owner. To relieve the debt, the sawmill owner cut down our trees and milled them at his mill in Angola. Many other neighbors had been very generous at this time. The Gier's provided a home in the upper floor of their huge farm house a couple miles from our farm. After the fire, most of our family lived there until the newly built house was ready in the fall. The Gier's became very good friends who provided transportation to the Lutheran Church in Gowanda for Johanne and the girls.

Digging the well was a challenge. We relied on a diviner to find water. Lorne had a knack for this. With a soft wood branch from the willow tree, he formed an inverted "Y" by grasping the two legs of the branch and turning both hands out and facing up. With the base of the "Y" now pointing up, Lorne traversed a likely spot to find water. When the tension laded branches sensed water below the surface, it would point down. Just outside the cellar wall was great, and so said the divining stick. We did not have to dig deep before we hit shale and water. Then the walls caved in. We had to build a box to retain the walls and support the upper earth. We capped the well nicely with a stone masonry mound. Later we learned that a well should be round. Unfortunately our water would be "hard." Now, I would be hard pressed to describe hard water. I do know that I prefer it.

We had brought our cistern over from the old house into which we collected really soft water, rain water. It flowed off the roof into this huge open wooden barrel whose staves were banded together by iron rods around its seven-foot diameter. Being five feet high it collected plenty of water. Soft water is great for rinsing soap from shampooed hair.

The sewer system also had to accommodate a floor drain and the double sink in the cellar, which was a big step up when it came to laundry. Our sewer system would have a septic tank and another boxlike transferral for the floor line. I am not sure what that wooden box was for. Maybe it served as a check valve. Installing the sewer system was no problem at all, except when it came to the septic tank. Putting the tank into a hole more than six feet deep was no problem. Unfortunately before any water was added to the tank, it rained all night. By morning the tank had floated up, out of the ground as the rain water created a pool at the bottom of the hole.

One more drain feature was incorporated into the house, although I am not sure it was connected to a sewer drain line. Around the outside perimeter of the foundation we laid drainage tubes. This is a very practical measure and may be required by code, although I do not think we went about building a house with any concern for building codes. The unique thing about this drain was the materials used in its construction. For some time there was a curious pile of paper tubes stacked in the yard. We understood at the time they were shipping tubes for artillery shells. How Far, or maybe it was Carl, came about them remained a mystery.

On the first floor were four primary rooms of about the same size and a small bathroom. These rooms accommodated a large kitchen with a wood stove, a bright open master bedroom, and two living rooms. They had beautiful hardwood floors that we polished with paste wax, buffing the wax by dragging each other around on the polishing cloth. One was a formal room where the Christmas tree was placed in the middle of the room. In one corner was a pretty china-cabinet and in another was a piano. In the old house the piano was in the master bedroom. It probably was not the same piano, as Niels often bought pianos cheap. Sometimes they were just for firewood and scrap metal. The kitchen was used for dining at a heavy wood table. In one "living" room was built a stone fireplace in a corner with its back to the kitchen and the end of the house. Although it was a custom design with an electric blower from two vents, it provided insufficient heat for the whole house, being as inefficient as fire places have always been. So Bill installed a wood burning furnace in the basement with heat directed to the first floor only. It proved more than adequate for the whole house.

Modern home conveniences first appeared in the house we built. Surprisingly, we started out with a wood stove and converted to an electric range. We never had a dryer. An ice box was how we kept milk cold. Ice boxes work by sharing interior space with a huge chunk of ice. In the summer time an iceman would deliver blocks of ice which you paid for, of course. We had a radio that played quite well. Today it would be a classic resembling a jukebox for its size and shape. A radio was important to Niels' business. He listened to the market report and news daily. It was a time when everyone must be quiet.

We got one notable appliance, for entertainment only, a couple years after they became available, a television. I believe Carl came home with it, maybe in 1952. TVs at the time were extremely unreliable. The Buffalo stations were only twenty-five miles away and we got a fairly good picture with the antenna, which was strapped to the chimney and well above the roof. However, this TV exhibited the classic high-tech scourge of the time. The vertical hold function was an engineer's nightmare, a problem that caused the picture to roll. Far solved the problem with a big stick. No, he did not trash the TV. The stick was like a remote control for the vertical hold adjustment. As sensitive as it was, a slight tap on the TV would bring the rolling picture to a halt. By banging the stick on the hardwood floor, enough shock was provided to simulate tapping the TV. Far lay on the couch to watch this new-age wonder and, with an old-age-measure, keep the ornery critter in line.

A stairway split the upstairs at the midpoint. There were four bedrooms and a hallway, large enough to serve as two bedrooms. The boys got one end of the top floor and the girls got the other. One bedroom was furnished with the least dust producing amenities available. It was Eugene's room. Edna and I slept in the hall/bedroom until the older children moved away either getting married or moving on.

For years, Johanne feared a repeat house fire. Hearing a noise in the chimney she summoned the fire department. As we came through Lawtons on our way home from school children yelled to at us that our "house was on fire." Fortunately, it was just the wind in the chimney. Just the same we paid close attention to the chimneysweep's task of cleaning the soot and tar from the flues by rattling a logging chain down the chimney.

Beyond that, a concern we should have had was the site that had been chosen for the new house. So close to the highway as it was, its location proved to be a danger.

"Dead Man's Curve"

For miles in each direction the highway made an unwavering path, straight across the land. Where it reached our farm it made an unexpected turn, a curve that caused more than a few to wish they had paid closer attention to the bend in the road. Some did not get another chance to pay closer attention to the road at Dead Man's Curve.

It was after the fire and our family was reestablished across the road in a newly constructed house. Unfortunately the house was set back less than fifty feet from the highway and there were no large trees for protection. We had not realized how much protection from the high speed traffic we would need. Three times this traffic made an unwelcome intrusion into our lives.

Johanne was cleaning the mirror in the parlor where Niels and his cronies had just begun to play pinochle in mid afternoon. Suddenly, she froze in panic. The sound of the crash seemed unreal as the surreal vision in the mirror unfolded, a horrifying scene of an automobile tumbling end over end straight toward our house. I was in the kitchen, not able to witness the accident, but hearing and sensing its calamity.

Rounding the bend, the unwary driver had lost control of his vehicle, a late model sedan. Two hundred feet farther his car left the pavement and dropped into our new orchard just missing the culvert at its edge. Tipped on its side, the car struck the rock reenforced embankment of our raised front lawn. Doors flew open; the driver was ejected, and the car flipped end over end in front of the house as the driver slid across the lawn on his shoulder, as later evidenced by a deep green stain on his jacket. The vehicle came to rest well past the lawn in the flower garden. The driver came to rest on the walkway to the house having dropped off the lawn at its opposite side. He had scraped his head on a sharp stone slab which formed the steps at the corner of the house.

Racing outside we found the driver sitting up with blood trickling down his face. Miraculously he was conscious and struggling to stand up. Surprisingly he was complaining that someone should so stupidly use a rock like that for their walkway. I wonder whether he ever thought later that his was the stupidity that caused his embarrassing introduction to that rock. Days later I found a Hamilton wrist watch in the barnyard. Even though it was slightly scratched, it worked well; I proclaimed it mine and wore it for years. Some months later my brother Bill wished for the watch to be his. That is when we figured it must have come from the man who made an uninvited stop on our front lawn.

Another time it was dark and damp as the cool spring air struggled to melt the last of the snow. This time we heard the screeching tires of a car skidding and the crunching crash as it came to a sudden stop. The lights in our house flickered and before we dashed out to see what had happened, we knew what this car had hit. The electric pole, a hundred feet south of the house, was sheered off. The power pole was suspended on two wires and miraculously electricity continued to flow. One wire had been dislodged from its condenser and sagged to only a few inches above the ground.

Although unaware of the drooping power line, we approached the scene cautiously. The offending vehicle had come to rest well clear of the pole and upright on the wet grass of the old hay field. The driver was not injured and unlike the prior intruder, he was embarrassed enough to apologize for the disturbance he had caused. It was not until the next day that we realized how close we had come to tripping over the downed power line when we raced back to our house.

The most memorable incident, at our notorious curve, was a tragic accident. It was three o'clock in the morning. Was I dreaming or awake and hearing this tragedy unfold? With the window open on a hot night just before high school graduation, we heard the speeding car go whizzing by, then the sudden crash. I bolted upright in bed and listened to the wheels still spinning and the horn blaring. My brother, Bill sprang up too. In unison our words spilled out, "It's an accident." We jumped out of bed, quickly dressed and headed out the door. We knew just where the accident had occurred, at our infamous curve, now Dead Man's Curve.

It was the first time I had ever seen a dead body. There were three. Two bodies with bare backs were visible as we approached the wreck. One on top of the other, they were wrapped around the seat back and wedged tight by the door post. The third body was in the back seat. I could not see it. I had seen enough and could not stand to go any closer. I did not see any blood. Years later I would understand that blood stops gushing when a heart stops beating.

Although we did not need him to tell us what had happened, there was one survivor. The young folks had been celebrating the successful completion of high school by one of the victims, an Indian girl who had excelled academically, an inspiration to her community. They had been drinking beer, had stayed until the bar closed. Now it was late and there was still another day of school. They should hurry home. What other factors may have contributed to their tragic end? There was at least one—the infamous bend in the road. The curve had now left a curse.

I was thirteen years old. I did not sleep more that night. I went to school and shared my still fresh vision of the tragedy. Later, in art class James Wells asked me how much blood was in our body. I said, "None." I thought he had asked how much blood was *on* those bodies. The scene stayed in my mind for months. Before this accident I had walked home, around that curve, hundreds of times, day or night. It was five years before I could walk past Dead Man's Curve after dark.

JBT 10/2005

Calamities struck by natural means as well.

"Thunder and Lightning"

Relief from our summer heat usually came in a sudden, dramatic way. This storm, we could see coming. To the west dark clouds were building fast. A cool breeze was stirring the air. It would be a welcome change if we did not get soaked in the approaching downpour. If I was to ride my bicycle home from the Harkness farm, where I was helping harvest their hay, it was certain that I could not beat the storm. Robert Harkness suggested that we put my bicycle into his car and he would drive me home that one mile down the road. With a healthy sense for haste, we made the trip and quickly I was safely in the house, dry and appreciative.

Now I could watch the storm as we always did on these occasions. Lightning and thunder was an intriguing spectacle that nature provided free, in a time of little else for exciting entertainment. Great viewing spots for the show were at a window or on the veranda. To feel like you were in the thick of the action, we often sat in the family car, where we also contemplated the safety of the viewing site we had chosen. We tracked nighttime storms by counting the time that elapsed time between the flash of lightning and its corresponding thunder crack, measuring its distance from us as about a mile for each five-second delay. Daytime thunder and lightning storms seemed to occur seldom and were less violent. Although the dark sky looked really ominous, I did not expect this storm to produce a significant spectacle. I was going to get a big surprise!

Having beaten the raindrops by seconds, I took up a post at the kitchen sink where a good sized window provided a full view of the barnyard. At that moment the sky opened up and let down a torrent of rain like I had never seen. Instantly water was gushing down the steep inclined pathway at the door to the milk house and flowing down the gentle grassy slope to the newly dug pond. In spite of the heavy downpour, daylight provided a clear view of the barn with its attached milk house which was less than seventy-five feet away. Suddenly my Mother and I were enveloped in a crash of sound and a flash of light. Shingles burst from the peak of the roof on the barn and fell onto the driveway. Lightning must have struck the lightning rod on the front end of the barn. Had we just observed how essential these old-fashioned farm features were? A thick braided copper cable that was attached to the lightning rod and extended to the ground was intended to short to the ground the lightning's electrical fury. How well had it done its job?

No sooner had we exchanged the realization that "lightning struck the barn," than we observed flames flickering in the milk house. I did not need to be told that this development demanded action! Without donning boots or any outer cover whatsoever, I dashed out to see what I could do to halt the flames. Our farm was no longer used for dairy production where a milk house provided natural refrigeration for milk until it was trucked away in a day or two. Thick concrete flooring and concrete vats fashioned in the floor and half filled with water provided the cooling at no cost. We used our dirty old milk house for storage and quick access to grease, oil, and a can of gas. The cool concrete provided the safest place possible for storing flammable fuels.

Reaching the milk house, I found the can of gas had tipped over and flames were licking up the leaking fuel. Although I realized that water was not the recommended combatant for a fuel fire, I had no better idea of how to arrest the flames. I grabbed a bucket and ran to the pond, slipping and sliding the hundred and fifty feet down the grassy slope. My last slip was right into the fresh mud rising in the water, as the rainwater carried me down the slippery slope. I dug myself out of the mud and swooped up a full pail of water. Then it was back up the grade with three steps forward and one back. By the time I reached the milk house the bucket was only half full. I found the flames not much different from before. With one heave I tossed the pail of water onto the fire. Out of the bucket came as much mud as water and with that the flames were smothered.

I returned to the house, so soaked by the rain that there was barely a sign of the mud bath that I had just taken. Later we noted that a lone tree, several hundred feet from the barn, had also been struck by the lighting and fractured. Although we surmised that the lightning's current had traveled along the electric fence back to the barn, it's more likely that the lightning bolt split its force between the tree and those ever attractive lightning rods. In a couple days the hay field was dry. When we got back to the harvest, Robert and I had a good laugh about how his effort to keep me dry had gone for naught on the day of thunder and lightning.

JBT 8/2006

Bill, the oarsman; Eugene, relaxed at the helm. I don't know who the coxswain is. In the background are hay loaders. The house on the right is at the infamous bend in the road.

"The Pond"

It was in the springtime that I noticed how wet the ground had stayed, just off from the farm-well where the water had strayed, when the well overflowed.

Dam up the leak, collect the water, and, when it freezes, I would have a great ice rink.

Near to the house, it would save that long-hike down to the swamp, where reeds though the ice often caused a skater to trip.

Digging wet turf, one shovel load at a time, was not like playing in the sand. I was saved when George Harkness stopped by, looking to hire a hand.

Ma pointed him to the boy, who was digging a pond. Mr. Harkness first admired my work and then he made an offer I could not refuse.

If I was willing to work as hard as it seemed, he would pay quite well this day for less toil on his farm.

My pond could wait for the machine it would take.

While I would go off, for a few dollars to make. George never suggested how foolish was my way, to think that, with just a spade in hand, a pond there could be some day.

I don't recall what farm work there was that day? The reward now is to recall my rescue from such folly, to dig, by hand, a pond? In the end the digging was left to a bulldozer.

JBT 10/2006

Call it Farming?

I never think of our farm as a producing farm. It was farmland and we raised a few crops so you could call it farming. The crops were all used for our horses and cattle. I remember one year we grew oats in a lumpy field that allowed the neighbors a good laugh. It was planted by Niels' Old World way, called broadcasting, easier to demonstrate than describe. (Try this: Place your arm in a sling; now take it out; fill the sling with grain. Reach into the sling for a handful of seed, dribble a few as you swing your arm back, now cast the rest to the front as you proceed across the field trying to remember where you were when the seed ran out.) It was a successful crop. The dirt clots melted in the rain.

We picked up good sized stones every spring, after the frost had pushed up a new crop. Frost also pushed up the fence posts. Pounding them back down was the first order of spring business, before the cows and horses could be let out to pasture.

Niels had plenty of friends to help on special occasions. Some were just good friends; others may have owed him for a favor he had done for them. At harvest time an old friend from Angola way came with a thrashing machine and steam tractor with steel wheels. It was a long way to drive without rubber tires. This may have been the same year we had corn that was allowed to ripen. Crows took their share at the end of the field by the swamp. The corn was added to the oats at the mill. First we husked the ears of corn, a task that made tender young hands sore. Before we took the corn to the grist mill to be ground and mixed with the oats, we stripped the kernels from the cob in a tool that consisted of a big flywheel and a hand crank. Now, turning the crank to see how fast we could make that wheel go was fun.

I think this "year of most success" was when Lorne took a leading role in farming. If we all had some aptitude for farming, it was Lorne whose ability stood out. He had the strength, desire and moxie. One year he raised some white face calves for the beef market, quite profitably. Far was generous to donate the space in the barn for this herd.

Niels was the only man around who planted buckwheat. Buckwheat was hardy and outgrew and suppressed weeds. We even grew corn across the rail road tracks one year as we tried to clear this land from the creeping forest brush. The brush soon regained the upper hand as getting across the swamp proved difficult. A bridge of railroad ties was never finished. Draining the swamp to some degree proved difficult with a horse and plow. The ground was saturated with water lily roots the size of a man's arm. These tough rots were able to tear the plow out of Far's hands.

Gardening

We had a vegetable garden and a large patch of potatoes and some tomatoes. You could get a lot of tomatoes from a small patch. We tried to grow melons. The watermelons were small. Muskmelons seemed to do a bit better. Sweet corn did well on our land though. We grew enough to sell by the roadside. The year Far and Ma spent the summer in Denmark, we tried several acres of sweet corn in a commercial venture—then got ripped off by a buyer.

Otherwise, generally I think our whole gardening endeavor was not worth a good cheer. The one exception I recall is asparagus. In the middle row of the garden Far planted the asparagus and covered it generously with straw and cow manure. Just as the tip of the plants broke through their dung heap he removed enough cover to reveal the thick white stalks and clipped them off. You have not tasted gourmet asparagus until you have a stalk that has not yet seen a ray of sun.

Beside the "new house" Niels tried some peach trees. I hoped to enjoy their delicious produce and wanted them to be huge, like the peaches that we purchased at unheard of prices on our trips to Canada. Ours were not so successful; the trees grew well enough, but their fruit was sparse. More success came from the current bushes we had transplanted from the garden at the "old house." The tiny red berries from these bushes were a pain to pick, unlike the larger variety in Denmark that are used for Jutlanders' favorite dessert, "*rød grød med fløde.*" It was becoming clear how much Niels and Johanne yearned for their homeland. Now, their growing of currants seemed to be a wishful transplantation of a "bit of Denmark."

Working on Our Farm

Although there were a couple of characters who hung out at our place from time to time, the children provided all the help that was needed on the farm. One was named Harold who later showed up again when Johanne was bedridden. I do not know where he stayed. I do remember an "Old Black Joe" who made his bed in the hay loft. He smoothed a stack of hay and covered it with a horse blanket with extra care.

The only thing I hated doing was milking cows. I was never good at it. I was not strong enough. Even today, I do not think I ever got strong enough. Here again I think of Lorne as the champion. Once we had seven cows at one time, if for only a short time. They had to be milked twice a day. That meant milking cows before going to school. Although she was rarely required to do so, Johanne was also very good at milking cows.

A challenging woodpile

One of the big jobs was collecting firewood for the cooking stove and in the winter for heat, first in the old pot belly stove in the old house, then the fireplace in the new house, and finally for the furnace that Bill installed in the new house. "Women have babies; men have trees." Far took his tree work seriously. Although we sometimes got slab wood from the saw mill, Niels never missed an opportunity to garner firewood when it was there for the taking, or so it seemed.

A mile down the highway, some huge Elm trees had been cut because of Dutch Elm Disease, a scourge that wiped out most of the stately Elms of New England. As these trees were alongside the road, it might be debated just whose trees they were. Regardless, when Far and I went to pick up the branches that were not too big for us to handle, the owner of the nearby farm came over and, without a word of greeting, asked what we were doing. Although it seemed quite clear we were gathering firewood, we did not go back for a second load.

Over the railroad tracks was a secluded stand of trees that had not been farmed in years. They belonged to a farm on the road behind our farm, about a half mile from their barn. Numerous dead logs lay just beyond the fence. The fence had long since fallen and was not even visible. So Far and I hooked a chain around the logs, one at a time, and attached the logging chain to a team of horses. Through the brush and stumps and over the hidden fence, the horses burst out of that thicket dragging the logs and Far too. Then we went about loading the logs onto our wagon. With a big log roller we managed to get a few up the slide ramp. One last, big log was one too many for us; half way up the ramp the big log started to slide back, increasing momentum as it came down. If Far could not slip his body past the end of the log, it would roll right over him and crush him. He saved himself by another trick. As the log slide down, he threw himself over the log and let it roll under himself. Realizing how cleverly he had saved himself, he nodded and we both smiled, surprised, happy and proud. He was sixty clever years old and remarkably spry.

I cannot say that I liked farming, or farm work, although I really liked "haying it."

"Haying It"

"Jim, come on. Let's go." Bonnie's insistent beckoning fractured my moment of nostalgic daydreaming. Watching the Amish farmers harvesting their crop of hay, my mind had carried me back fifty years to a day when I was fourteen years old. It's a day that I have thought back upon many times. The Amish farmers are still using the same equipment, the same method I had known on our farm in Western New York in the dying days of draft horses as farm machines. Far insisted on farming the old way. We used horses in lieu of a tractor. Heavy tractors laid a constant track on the earth, excessively packing it down.

The Amish horses pulled a hay wagon, a wagon with a flat bed to which was attached a hay loader just like the one we used. The hay loader operates like a conveyor with a rake to push loose hay six to seven feet up onto a wagon. The partially dry hay had been gathered into long lines called windrows. When the hay loader is pulled over the windrow, it rakes up the hay and pumps it out like a stream of water from a hose. The Amish are probably the only farmers still harvesting hay this way. Bailing was the new method in the 1950s. Bailed hay today is even more different from those early bails were from loose hay. We never converted to bailed hay. Far could not abide feeding a condensed food packet of bailed hay to his stock.

Harvesting hay was my favorite farm work. When the hay was ripe in early summer and it seemed like no rain would occur for five days, we took on this task full bore. We referred to our project as "haying it." I loved "haying it." The sweet smell of fresh-cut hay, loose and drying, has an allure that tickles my senses even today. However, bailed hay loses that inviting smell. I even liked the sweat, dust, and grime. The leather harness, slapping against the horses, lathered up their sweat which amplifies their musky smell of strength and stamina. In turn, it amplified my motivation for a long day of hard labor. When the hay dust brought on a good healthy sneeze, I exaggerated the effort for a better healthy sneeze, lifting my spirit as I cleared my nose. With a sense of pride I cleansed my sweaty coat of grime and bid farewell to a day of hard earned pleasure.

That day which I remember so fondly actually began the night before. My best friend David Aeschbacher, who lived about a mile away, had inherited his grandfather's farm. Because his farmhouse was just a shout away from his parents' house, he was allowed to sleep there occasionally. We did so regularly in the summer and occasionally in the winter, although we had no heat. On this evening we stayed up late as usual, and even later. In fact, we did not go to sleep at all. To Far and Ma's surprise, I had walked home early. To my surprise I was ready to work. There would be only Far and me available for a day of "haying it."

I had given a little thought to whether I would have enough energy for a day of my favorite work. I had given a lot of thought to how I could keep secret that I had not slept. I would resort to a magic potion, chocolate milk. I started the day with some toast and a big glass of chocolate milk. Far had already harnessed the horses. After we hooked up the wagon and hay loader, we headed to the hay field.

In the field I drove the team and Far layered the streaming hay onto the wagon in a deft manner to extend the width of the load. The technique used to keep this widened load from sliding back to the ground required a skill I had not yet mastered. To keep from being buried by a haystack, as the hay piled up, I climbed higher up a tenuous ladder. When we had a full load, it was my job to unhook the loader from the wagon. That meant two treacherous trips on the back side of that tenuous ladder and bare inches behind the horses' hind hooves.

Reaching the barnyard I slid off the wagon while it was still rolling, ran to the house, and quickly drank a big glass of chocolate milk. Then I ran back to the barn where Far was getting ready to unload our crop. With uncommon teamwork we pulled off this detailed process without a hitch—not exactly. Far had unhitched the horses from the wagon and rehitched them to a tackle arrangement which was used to lift the hay off the wagon. I stabbed a grapple fork into the hay and climbed out of the way. Far led the team so they pulled smoothly, lifting the hay until the grapple latched into a trolley at the top of the barn. The trolley flew along its rail until it reached the place where each load was to be dropped. Yanking on the trip rope, I ceremoniously released the grapple hooks with a shout, "Trip it!" This symbolic phrase vocally announced the successful employment of our mechanics.

Then my work really began. We called it "mowing hay." Mowing the hay well makes it easier to remove in the winter to feed the stock. It was important to keep the hay filling up in level layers and eliminate knots and gnarls. These problems were fewer when the hay dropped farther, floating down like a parachute. With a pitch fork I would push, pull, lift and carry the hay to the sides of the hay "mow." Walking through a fresh layer of loose hay is like wading through waist-deep water. To get a picture of the full effort which was needed imagine wading through water carrying another fifty pounds on your shoulder.

Then it was back to the wagon for another grapple load. It could take six repetitions to empty the wagon. Before we headed back to the hayfield, I downed another swig of chocolate milk. Far refreshed himself with a beer.

Reattaching the hay loader to the wagon deserves some description. Imagine backing your car into your garage. Now imagine backing your boat trailer attached to your car into your garage. Now replace your car with a team of horses, and get them to back your boat trailer into the garage. Far could manage it well even with the most stubborn team. I provided a minimum of guidance to close the wagon hook to the hay loader's towing tongue.

This is the way it went all day as Far and I were "haying it" together. Get a load of hay; get some milk; unload the hay; get some milk. To make it through the day I had drunk more than a gallon of chocolate milk. We took in seven loads of hay that day, a record. Even with a full farm-family crew we had never gotten so much haying done in one day. I was pretty proud of myself. I think Far was pretty proud of us too. Unlike ever before, that night he made mention of our achievement. Ma hid a slight smile of understanding, knowing that there must be a secret reason for my many dashes for chocolate milk. I never told a soul I had not slept the night before.

In my youth Far and I worked together a few other times. None of them stayed in my memory, like the day just the two of us "hayed it" together. I never got to tell him that I had not slept the night before. I never got to tell him how much that one day meant to me.

JBT 10/2005

Family Dinner Fare

Johanne did not have a favorite dish that she made. Everyday Ma baked, not just bread, but at least a coffeecake as well. Some dishes may have had a Danish flavor. I think it was more out of wishing it than making it so. Niels and Johanne often disputed how one Danish dish was made, seldom reaching agreement. That was even true for a popular Danish food that Ma prepared frequently, *frikadeller*, fried meat balls. I do remember Far saying, "I want restaurant food."—Somewhat in jest, I hope. Johanne did make *klijner*, a Christmas pastry. Others helped, even Far; he took charge of dropping the dough into the hot grease, turning the pastries and retrieving them. What amazed me was that Ma, more perfectly than anyone, could slice the dough into diamonds, just the right size. Bonnie now also makes some Danish foods which I do not recall Ma making, like *æbleskiver*, a ball-like pancake for which you need a special skillet.

Bread pudding was a common dessert because by making it, Ma kept extra bread, that may have gotten dry, from going to waste. Rice pudding was an economical dish to serve and curried rice, so far from her ethnicity, was also a starch staple. When wild berries were in-season Ma made the best elderberry and wild blackberry pies. We found these berries right beside old Wilcox Road at the corner of our farm. They also made a fine dish to serve at coffee time to anyone who happened to stop by. Johanne and Niels' "afternoon coffee" was a tradition that welcomed friends and neighbors without the need for a special occasion. Many of their children enjoy the same coffee-time tradition today.

Sunday dinner was the one big meal of the week. It usually meant a roast of chicken. There may also be pork chops or ham. In the best of times a roast of veal or goat was a real treat. A couple of carefully chosen holes were sliced in the goat roast and stuffed with parsley. This was the favorite meal for many. Home canned peaches or pears topped off the Sunday meal.

We learned at a very young age that wastefulness, when it came to food, would not be tolerated. Ma would always say, "Clean your plate so we will have good weather tomorrow." That was a kinder way to say, "You eat what you take," which meant you do not leave the table until your plate is empty.

Niels bought in-bulk many items of produce and processed foods when a bargain could be had. Try finding peanut butter in a square shaped five-gallon can. After the war these bulk items were government surplus. Bulk produce at auctions is where we got the stuff for canning such as peaches, apples and strange fruits. Have you ever heard of a quince? We usually had enough beets, beans and tomatoes from our garden for canning. Before we had a refrigerator, Ma also canned and salted meat. The new house was well equipped for canning with a second stove in the basement, a lot of room, and a large table. A pressure cooker, as dangerous as the early ones seemed, was an essential appliance. Sugar, flour, spices, tea and coffee came from the grocery store. Later on we became more dependent on stores for food stuffs even including bread and butter.

It wasn't dinner fare. However, one food was unique to our home: brown sugar sandwiches. The children made these sandwiches for themselves for school lunches and when working at a farm job away from the house. Brown sugar was cheap, adding it to a sandwich made an inexpensive treat, especially when the sandwich had been in the hot sun until lunchtime and now the butter and sugar had melted to made a pastry as much as a sandwich.

Grilled mushrooms were a delicacy that was available in the Spring. Far would take an eight-quart basket with him to the pasture a couple days after a light rainstorm. These rectangular baskets were common and practical, although I have not seen one since then. Wild mushrooms would appear in the most fertile places, where cows had once left their mark. That is not why we feared eating this epicurean delight. We knew of annual reports of persons poisoned by mushrooms gathered in the wild. To ensure the safety of our fried mushrooms we added ten cents to the skillet. We understood that the poison would react with the silver in the dime if the mushrooms were poisonous. We were not sure, what the evidence of this reaction was to look like.

Elderberry pie was a treat that Ma made when that fruit ripened on the few bushes in the ditch along old Wilcox Road. We shared this harvest with our neighbor up the hill, Drew Griffin, old "Griff" to us. He often brought the berries for Ma to bake. Later in the summer we harvested fine wild blackberries from the same spot and shared them in the same manner. We had a huge patch of elderberry bushes in the lower field, but the red-winged blackbirds from the swamp feasted on them so well that there was never a pie to be had from that patch.

Beyond Farm Labor

Crafts and Cards: Johanne sewed out of necessity, mending rather than making. Being a homemaker with eight children was Ma's hobby. Surprisingly, she found time for the Home Bureau. In those days, Home bureaus were the Martha Stewart of today, a famous entrepreneur whose empire markets homemaking news and paraphernalia. One of the crafts that Johanne learned, or it was probably refreshing of an early skill, was caning, a craft that turned an old chair into a prized item. Most cane backed furniture goes back to that period. Surviving pieces are a treasure. Niels and Johanne went to card parties. I think Niels was impressed at "how good at cards she got."

Vacations: Before the family had grown to so many children, for vacations the older children enjoyed exchange visits with good friends who had been neighbors on the first of the rented farms. One child would stay for a week with the Janiks in Buffalo and one of the ten Janiks kids would visit on the farm. If the whole family was to go somewhere together, the big cattle truck was our limousine. The bigger kids would stand with only a toe hold on the hitching rings, being able to peer over the sides. Two or three of the youngest kids sat between Ma and Far in the cab. Later going places with Ma and Far just for pleasure probably only happened for Edna and me. We would go with Ma and Far to Canada to visit their very good friends. I think their name was Christensen. It was always a cool trip. One time we went in a coupe with only two seats. Edna and I stood behind the seats at a speed that probably never exceeded fifty miles per hour, a snail's pace, all the way to Toronto or its suburbs, a half day's journey. This trip also included a stop at Welland Canal that allows ocean vessels to go to Lake Erie and beyond. Of course, it held us up. It always took a long time to operate the canal locks to raise and lower the ships. The return trip from Canada usually included a stop at Niagara Falls for the spellbinding view of this most powerful waterfalls. Here, standing at the edge of the Falls, Niels regularly reflected on how the falling water seemed to hypnotize, as it tried to draw you into it.

Birthdays: I do not remember any birthday gifts or special foods. However, Ma made a cake with our name on it. The big celebrations, back then, were fund raisers for the Volunteer Fire Departments, the firemen's carnivals. Every fire station had them and coordinated their schedules so we never missed a one. I think we all looked forward to the day when we would be old enough to hang out at the beer tent. About the time that day came for me, these carnivals became a thing of the past.

Church? Niels wanted no part of it. I think that Ma found her way to live a spiritual life with great satisfaction, particularly after the Lutheran Church in Gowanda became available to her. Transportation was a big hurdle. She never drove a vehicle. I do not recall that Far took her to church nor did she ask him. I do believe that if she had asked, he would have taken her (and waited outside). We were sent to Sunday school and church, one was the Congregational Church in North Collins. We would get a ride from one of the many "missionary" types in the area.

Discipline: "Children should be seen; not heard." Niels was a "strict disciplinarian." The fear of a "good trashin" was adequate to assure the children's best behavior. I was about six years old when I learned my lesson. David, who would become my best friend, was visiting one afternoon. He had a balloon. I was envious and stuck a pin in his balloon. He tattled and I was punished. How? I was sent to bed with nothing to eat.

However, both Niels and Johanne had playful sides. Niels had lost part of a finger in a mining accident. Every child who sucked its thumb was shown what happened to him when he sucked his thumb. The child was impressed, if only for a moment.

"To Catch a Deer"

When we were so young and enthralled with the beauty of the animal kingdom, not long before Walt Disney made his famous animated feature, *Bambi*, it was common to tell children about how to catch a deer. Of course we wanted so badly to catch a deer that we never gave a thought to the possibility that we were being teased. It sounded so easy. "To catch a deer simply put some salt on its tail. When the deer turned to lick the treasure from its tail (which it could do easily), you simply slip a rope around its neck," Far would say, with an undetected "tongue in check." The older children quickly picked up on this suggestion and reinforced my vision of achieving such a goal.

The occasion to make an attempt at this practice came one bright morning in early summer. The older children were off to school. Edna and I were playing in the yard when we spied on the hillside only five hundred feet away a small herd of white tail deer including a couple of spotted fawns. With due excitement we pointed out our discovery to Ma and stated our desire to catch one of those cute creatures. Surprisingly, Ma said, "Well, you know how. Get a rope and go after them." I am sure she thought we would give up as soon as the deer raced off when they sensed our approach. That never occurred to me.

A rope was easy enough to find in the shed. A single shake of salt into one hand should be enough to do the trick. Then we were off up the hillside and soon beyond the bounds that we had ever before exceeded. Sure enough the deer caught our scent and bounded away. I would not be deterred, and we continued in pursuit through ever taller weeds and past the tree line. Now the house was out of sight. However, we could still see the highway and never thought about our becoming lost. Across a creek and then a small meadow, we entered the forest and skirted its edge as we pressed on further from home. Tiring a bit midway to the end of a freshly turned field we came upon a shed. This shed deserved exploration.

Among the loose boards which served as a floor, what should we find but the largest potatoes we had ever seen. The farmer, Harkness was his name, had overlooked these fine specimens. All thoughts of catching Bambi vanished. We would bring home this bonanza for a just reward. Picking up the largest potato each hand would hold, we set off straight down the hill toward US Highway 62 and a shortcut home.

Perhaps Ma thought it was about time for us to be back. Ma tells how when she looked out she saw traffic backed up on the highway. Leading the parade of vehicles was a Greyhound bus. Ahead of the bus in the middle of the road came the grand marshals, Edna and I, with our hands clutching huge potatoes. I do not remember walking in the middle of the road. Surely, the bus was a deserved escort.

JBT 11/2005

At Christmastime

Gifts: Gifts were hand made if there were any. Ma knitted mittens and wrist "warmers," a garment that covered just the wrist and was designed and made only by Johanne. This was the rationale for these extra unobtrusive garments: Here the blood was close to the skin, extra protection extended its warmth keeping the hands warm longer and hands naturally free. They worked great, if the air temperature was not much below freezing.

Yuletide: We probably came closest to experiencing Danish heritage at Christmas. I remember once being dressed in a green elf outfit and sitting on the stairs behind the door. I did not realize I was portraying *yule niesse*, the Danish elf that hides in the attic and puts presents in your shoes at Christmas. Johanne would make rather dull looking Christmas wreaths with moss, binding it tightly to a wire hanger by wrapping the moss stems around the hanger with piano-like wire. The wreaths were gifts for neighbors. The Christmas tree was our most evident ethnic symbol, being erected on Christmas eve and decorated with candles. It stayed up for weeks until all the neighbors and friends had seen it with candles lit.

Christmas celebrations were largely uneventful except for the food, a delightful dinner of a delicious roast goose on Christmas eve.

"The Christmas Goose"

"Christmas is a Comin'"

"Christmas is a comin' and the geese are gettin' fat."
I'm a gonna do somethin' 'bout that.
They've been a rootin' and they've been a tootin'.
All summer long they've been a hootin', (Honkin' that is.)
They've been a goin' here, and they've been a goin' there;
They've been a droppin' stuff everywhere. (Watch your step.)
They ain't a mindin' no fence . They're just a big nuisance.
And they've a got me on the defense.
Now I'm a gonna spare you the last line of this ditty,
'Cause it's a not that witty and it ain't very pretty.
However, if you insist I won't resist.
Then I'll be a tellin' ya', how I'm a gonna slay da' fella.
Oh, what the heck, I'll just wring his neck.

A roasted goose on the table for Christmas dinner was a treat as much as it was a tradition. Getting that treat to the table was like a year-long nightmare. The little bird that pecks its way out of its egg after three weeks of confinement has not exactly developed into an ugly duckling. A middle cousin between a duck and a swan, the goose has adopted the worse character of each.

Although there was one gosling that I took a shine to and he to me, geese generally make poor pets. They are an independent lot, happy to take a handout without a word of appreciation. In fact what you are likely to get at feeding time is a threatening rebuke for having come too near. These birds seem to be in a perpetual threat mode, attacking with outstretched neck and wings raised high.

For the goose's so called master, there can be a plus side to their antagonistic nature. They are quick to warn of an intruder.

However, if they happen to be nosing around the front yard when an invited guest approaches, you may need to rescue the guest with the sweep of a broom. At minimum a frequent guest will have learned a sidestep shuffle that allows forward progress while keeping a cautious eye to the harassing honkers.

Just like we wanted, our geese plumped up nicely in the fall. Their regular forays into the corn field to steal a sumptuous meal hastened their growth and sealed their doom. Another reason you want a nice fat goose is that a big fat goose cannot fly and will be around at harvesting time—his harvesting that is. Once around the barn is the longest flight I ever saw our geese take. More than that and they would get their wings clipped. Just a couple inches painlessly cut from their longest feathers quickly put an end to their airborne antics.

A week or so before Christmas it was time to take a toll of our gaggle. Although we only sold this prized dinner entree to our neighbors and European friends, geese were the only cash-crop that we raised. I could easily catch the victims once we stood our ground. When they hesitated and turned away, one quick grab for any part of the goose usually meant its capture. Then a tight grip of both wings was in order to preclude a thorough spanking from them. However, your battle is not over; your captive's calvary was coming to the rescue. With no hand available for our usual broom shield, the goose in hand would do for a defensive sweep. Once when I repelled the onslaught a little too aggressively, Ma scolded me, "Tsk, Tsk, there's no need for that!"

Plucking the feathers from the big bird is where the work begins. Unlike scalding a chicken to pluck its feathers, geese are plucked while their feathers are dry. We wanted the down feathers to remain dry and fluffy to fill our pillows and a feather bed quilt. You pulled most of the feathers by taking a few at a time between thumb and index finger and quickly yanking them in the opposite direction from their natural lay. The big wing feathers were pulled straight out one at a time. Before long, your fingers are plenty sore and your biggest challenge is still ahead.

Rarely could the tufts of down be pulled out without tearing the goose's tender hide once or twice. To limit the damage the process becomes even more painstaking. Some of the blemishes blended out while the goose ripened in the cellar for a few days.

Speaking only from experience, I would say that, cooking a goose, is similar to roasting any bird. Any good carving knife is all you need to divvy up a portion. We used a unique pair of scimitar-shaped scissors that could chop right through bones. Cut the breast laterally (not the way you carve a turkey). We stuffed our goose with dried prunes and apple chunks in lieu of bread-stuffing. Goose grease does not do much for croutons. A roasted goose produces a generous amount of grease. Good old goose grease, for some, it was a bread-spread, better than butter. Far's fancy for it I could understand, being from that generation and the old country; as for my brothers, I am not sure. And me? I prefer butter.

Speaking of goose grease, a word of caution: It ignites at the temperature needed to roast a goose. Since those days on the farm, Bonnie and I have bought a goose for Christmas a few times. Only once did our oven become aflame—the last time. Fortunately I was able snuff the fire out by pressing the oven door closed. Now our tradition is just a dream, albeit, one we relive every year.

JBT 11/2005

"Christmas Trees"

In mid November with major shopping malls erecting their holiday centerpiece and entrepreneurs establishing Christmas tree lots here and there about town, I am reminded of a Christmas tree tale or two.

The oldest of these memories is of my first Christmas tree. It takes me back to my first year in school, when I had just turned five years old. Beginning our walk home from school we crossed the highway and there in Harkness' front yard stood newly cut Christmas trees. I had no idea they were "For Sale." I was sure one was meant for me and headed straight to a perfect tree that was a little taller than I. I did not really ask; I just presumed I was to be given this tree. Mr. Harkness knew what was on my mind and led us to the back, to a lot of trees behind his house. There he suggested a second rate tree that was the same size. Apparently being a good judge of Christmas trees, I insisted on the dandy one that I had first spied in the front yard.

With the free tree held proudly in hand, we set off for the last mile home. To my surprise, as I carried the tree, it grew; at least it got heavier. Soon I could carry it no further. Fortunately Robert and Wally (Walter), the Jentz boys, who were my age and much bigger, were willing to share the burden. At their house I took over and lugged the precious fir the last quarter mile. I arrived home anticipating a rousing welcome for acquiring such a fine Christmas tree. To my surprise I was to receive no such greeting; instead I was to learn all about the commercial part of the Christmas season. Immediately, Ma was on the phone to the Harkness', thanking them for their understanding and insisting on paying for the tree. I am sure George and Eva Harkness declined any compensation. They would rather bank the memory of a child's delight at gaining a gift that is still so memorable.

Years later I would learn much more about the Christmas tree business. On the hillside by our house I would help Mr. Harkness plant a new crop of fir trees. Unlike the popular Christmas tree farms of today with their manicured trees planted in precise rows after the ground has been properly cultivated and enriched with expensive fertilizer, the Harkness enterprise was very organic.

We did have an efficient tree planting process though. With a handful of seedlings I followed Mr. Harkness' adult son, Robert, as he cut through a matted layer of tangled grass and pressed a spade into the damp earth. Tipping the spade forward Robert widened the crack so I could slip a seedling into the slot. I held the seedling in the ground while Robert pressed the sticky soil off the spade with one foot. Adding a little more weight to his step, Robert sealed the plant in its natural pot. Two paces forward, we repeated the process and continued until we had planted a hundred trees in a couple hours. In a couple years an impressive grove of Christmas trees graced the hillside.

The Harkness' were treasured people in my life. Again years later we would share trees of a different nature, our family trees. My wife, Bonnie, is their niece.

If Far or Ma did pay for that first tree, it was the only Christmas tree they ever bought. Because, for our tree we would go into the woods a couple days before Christmas to find a tree that nature had planted. Finding a flawless tree was impossible, and cutting branches, drilling holes in the green tree trunk, and tying on branches to fill gaps was a frustrating experience. I do not feel so bad now, having read that the two-hundred-foot tall, perfect tree at the upscale shopping center, Fashion Island, is assembled by cutting up to five hundred branches and wedging them into holes drilled in the tree trunk in the same way we fixed our tree. To stand it upright, we wedged our tree into a home made concrete spool. Our holiday centerpiece stood for over a month in the middle of the living room without a drop to drink, as seems so vital to Christmas trees today.

My last story of childhood Christmas trees is about the last tree I remember harvesting from nature. Our stock of nature's trees had dwindled as Far sold parcels of the farm. For this tree we went onto a neighbor's farm. In Ernie's open pasture was the perfect Christmas tree, a tree we had eyed for years. We needed only six feet of this forty-some-foot tree. Not realizing how it jeopardized the tree's health to say nothing of destroying its stately appearance, we took that six feet right off the top. From the ground it appeared to be a perfect tree; once on the ground we found that our perfect tree's top six feet were not so perfect. Another night of tree construction was in a store.

Of course Ernie noticed right away that his perfect tree had been, shall I say, altered. Knowing well the answer, he good-heartedly asked me, and he may have asked my brothers, if I knew who had topped his tree. In reply, I managed a shrug as something less than a denial or confession.

JBT 11/2005

Niels and Johanne's Danish Christmas Tree

Trust in their Children

Niels and Johanne granted the children considerable freedom and trusted them to behave, be careful, and stay out of trouble. They probably worried about their children to the same degree as all parents at that time, without letting on as to their concern. When it came to allowing the kids to go, by themselves, to the "Hamburg Fair" her word of caution exposed Ma's worry. Our freedom to roam made for fun years as we grew up in our rural environment.

Hiking was encouraged as a means of exercise to which Niels and Johanne related. Frequent hikes to the woods and swamp often led to discoveries that Ma was glad to hear about when we returned. One mid afternoon, I was returning from a walk up old Wilcox Road. Heading down the hill toward the West, I was struck by the color of the sky. It had the most unusual pinkish hue I had ever seen. Although I felt it must be caused by discharge from the steel mills in Buffalo, I asked Ma what she thought. She did not disagree. Then she told how, when she was a child the sky had once, only once, turned to a strange color like it was this day. She recalled that it was at the time of the Miracle of Fatima when some atmospheric phenomenon was observed over much of Europe. I felt she was not ascribing any divinity to her experience, rather taking the opportunity to suggest a parallelism to our lives.

As we got older, another fun thing was learning to drive. Johanne never drove any vehicle. She was a good judge of safe driving though. Niels always drove the car or truck, until one of the kids became old enough to learn. He did not provide any instruction; he just let the child take over. We learned to drive while riding with Far, maybe driving a neighbor's tractor and, taking a free driver's education class in high school.

Niels must have driven hundreds of thousands of miles for business, visiting friends, and on trips to Canada. He did have a couple of minor accidents. One night he took the youngest kids to the movie theater in North Collins to see one of Walt Disney's classic animated films. Turning the corner as he stopped the truck to let us out, the top of the truck raked the protruding theater marque. Out of the theater rushed the owner, a woman, and attacked Niels with the vilest verbal assault my five-year-old ears had ever heard. For Niels, perhaps this incident established a stereotypical view of many of the residents of North Collins and his dislike for them.

We gave ourselves some special driving lessons and practice. At the county fairs, we had seen the daredevil auto thrill shows and Joey Chitwood, a driver we most admired. It was when Niels and Johanne spent the summer in Denmark that we thought to emulate the thrill show stunts. It should have been enough just to turn the small hayfield near the house and along the highway into a race course. We sought more. So with an older car that ran well but was off the road, we raced around on the wet grass skidding and sliding looking for a dip and a rut to call a ramp. The kids filled the back seat and the neighbors filled the grandstand, the Munson's yard on the hillside.

We just could not get enough speed, so we moved to the neighbors hay field across the railroad tracks and out of sight. We achieved a straightaway speed of forty miles per hour and hung a hard left at the end of the dry field. The right front tire dug hard into a rut and ripped the wheel lugs right through the rim. It was an unforgettable lesson and a long walk home.

When I was learning to drive legally, I took the old green, retired, 47 Chevy for a trip down to the swamp. Heading out across the old corn field, I put on the speed and bounced joyfully over the old corn rows until the car stalled. I abandoned the old-faithful car, not knowing a fuel line had been jarred loose. Far was not pleased with my folly and that I had treated the former faithful family sedan like a dirt track thrill-show vehicle. Our real thrill show antics were kept a secret.

"Camping"

When I was in my mid teens, my oldest brother, Carl, came home with a tent, I mean a real tent, a four-man Army tent, a heavy, thick-canvas tent. I do not know how he came to have it. No one else seemed that interested, so when I immediately claimed it for myself, there were no complaints. With some help I set up my tent in the back yard. I installed a cot, and all summer long I slept in the tent.

Friends came for stay-overs and we slept in the tent. We did not always sleep. As long as flashlight batteries held out we might read detective magazines. They were popular in the fifties. Other times we might take a night hike. It seemed like an adventurous thing to do. One night, apparently we were a little too quiet. Being suspicious, Ma sent Bill out to see what we were up to. Of course he could not see what we were up to. We were not there. David and I had taken a walk about a mile down the road to a newly opened snack shack for some candy. Bill was waiting for us when we returned. At first we offered that we had just gone to the barn to check on a newly born calf. Sensing that Bill would back me up, I came clean and left it to him to assure Ma that all was okay.

Before the summer was over, why should I not really go camping? Although Ma probably had misgivings, permission was granted for Wally and me to spend a week about two miles away in a hollow by the creek on Quaker Road. Wally and I went to the supermarket with his mother for provisions. With little regard for storing the food, we got butter, eggs, bacon, and hotdogs as well as potatoes, bread, and canned beans. The load of food, clothes, cooking utensils, army tent, and bedding along with our bicycles fairly filled Far's cattle truck in which he transported us to the unofficial campsite on private property, the owner of which we had no idea. In seven days Far was to return to pick us up. Keep in mind: I never was a boy scout.

We set up the tent right next to the brook which could be a substantial stream in the spring. Although we had not given rising water any thought, now it was late summer and the risk was negligible. Everything had gone smoothly as we set about planning our adventure. We explored our surroundings looking for an easier path to lug our gear up to the roadway in a week. We cooked hotdogs, roasted on our first campfire. It was the main course that evening and others nights as well. Time passed quickly and soon it was getting dark.

Night sounds of familiar animals could now be heard. Then came sounds that were not familiar. Our minds whipped up visions of forest denizens. We recalled the reported sighting of a family of black panthers a few years earlier, less than a mile up the stream from where we were camping. I recalled the eerie sound that I had heard in the middle of the night a couple years subsequently. Having been told that the screech of the panther sounded like a woman crying, I was sure we had heard a panther. We decided it was "tent time"—a ritual pronouncement that we made for seven nights. The best thing about that old army tent was that it could be securely closed from the inside.

The week passed quickly and for the most part uneventfully. We hiked the stream from the camp site all the way to the old swimming hole under the railroad trestle about a mile downstream. On both sides of the creek were enticing cliffs that begged our effort to climb. In the stream was our only face-to-face encounter with animals. We played at spearing fish with sticks we had fashioned for the purpose. It was not the fish that caused excitement though. We were wading downstream barefoot in the brook right next to our tent, and swimming up the stream toward us, side by side, were two snakes. Speaking of sneaky snakes, these two really fit the bill. They were swimming underwater, a behavior that I had never before imagined or heard about. We stepped gingerly aside and exacted a certain, shall we say brutal revenge.

We took long bike rides, one to Zoar Valley, a popular site for camping and picnicking about ten miles away, returning by way of Buttermilk Falls and the town of Gowanda, where I went to school. Then there was the trip around the block, about ten miles, to investigate the old tree that blocked Rte. 39. The road made a sudden curve around it and local lore had it that a curse would befall anyone who felled the tree. Years later the tree was gone, and it is recorded in Guinness Records that this tree had a bank account. Perhaps financial ruin led to its demise. Another time we rode to Lawtons less than a mile from home, and had a hamburger at the Rainbow Inn that was once my one-room schoolhouse.

With snack bar stops here and there, we did not have to do as much cooking as we had anticipated. Our one culinary catastrophe was cooking the fresh whole potatoes, which we had brought. We could not keep water boiling long enough to cook them. Of course, looking back, we should have just tossed them into the fire. Hey, I never was a boy scout and I never had "hobo stew."

My first camping expedition was my last. Right on schedule Far returned and our adventure was complete.

JBT 01/2007

Confidence in their Children

It was a great day for them when Niels and Johanne got the opportunity for a family visit to Denmark. They were anxious to see their families who had endured years of German occupation during the Second World War. In spite of Niels and his family's meager existence, after the war he regularly sent "care" packages to his and Johanne's families. This generous act continued for several years. Mailing packages, which contained coffee, tea, sugar and spices, was an expensive way to supply staple items to war-torn Europe.

Their yearning for the homeland was tempered by the anxiety of leaving their children for their planned long stay in Denmark. Although finally convinced that the children would be okay and that now was the time to go, it took a determined tug from Uncle Jim and Aunt Thora to send them on their way with tears streaming, a most unusual sight as Niels and Johanne showed neither public emotion nor much physical affection. Open display of emotion was rarely observed in our childhood, at home or away. As children, we rationalized that this was the apparent norm for human behavior in their generation. (Children probably still assess their parents' normalcy by comparing notes with other kids.) The closest physical contact that the little children had with Niels was when they combed his hair. He enjoyed that and we often had fun combing his hair.

Niels and Johanne stayed in Denmark for five months and returned with cultural treasures filling thirteen pieces of baggage including trunks which protected their choicest treasures, thus reaffirming their proud heritage. Our home was completely redecorated and remained so until these prized symbols of Danish heritage were given to their children when each one married.

Heavy brass platter

Besides the Jacobsen paintings, two bed warmers and a heavy brass plate, emblazoned with the Danish Royal Seal, have been passed to me. Whether this brass platter was simply decorative or had a function was disputed, with Johanne disagreeing with Niels, whose contention was that the purpose of the platter was to provide a repository for the lit cigar of an arriving guest so the smoke-able stub could be retrieved upon departure.

The children were trusted to get along, make-do and work together while Niels and Johanne were in Denmark. Their confidence in them managing the farm was well placed. However, there was a bump or two in the road.

"Runaway Horses"

The first motor vehicle I ever drove was a farm tractor. It was only once, when I was recruited by the farmer next door to steer the tractor while he loaded hay bales on the wagon that was in tow. He set the throttle to walking speed. To get the tractor moving was easy because the clutch that engaged the drive train was operated by a long handle that moved easily and seemed to slip the clutch automatically. Pushing the clutch handle forward was all that was needed to stop. The wagon load brought the tractor to a halt without the driver having to hit the brakes. Operating the tractor was a simple task since the need to use your feet was eliminated. It was years before I drove another vehicle. We did not use a tractor on our farm.

Far insisted on the farming old way, with horses and harness. From early on, as all the boys did, I drove a team of horses. Far hefted the harness onto the team, hitched the farm implement to the harness, and sent us to the field. Cultivating the newly plowed earth to smooth it and break up the dirt for planting was the most common task that I was sent out to do alone. I walked behind a rake, called a drag, and drove the team, sometimes a trio of horses. It was work that offered fun as well. When grass and weeds would clog up around the rake's tines, a spritely step on the clog, while the horses were still pulling, could dislodge it; a misstep could almost dislodge your foot. Although I once sprained an ankle, it was the only time I regretted taking up that challenge. We used a diagonal route across the field then repeated the route adjacent to the first track making right turns only. Repeating this pattern, with the opposite diagonal, raked the soil three or more times and from different directions, an important factor. Just the same, our effort was not as successful as with more modern disking machines. One year our field for oats was so lumpy the neighbors chided us for such a result. However, a good rain and gravity somehow dissolved those lumps into a fine field of grain.

Finishing the day, when dealing with horses, presented its own issues. The horses are tired, thirsty, and want to go home. We cautioned ourselves that the horses needed a cool-down period, the same as we do after a physical workout. For fear of causing lameness we were not supposed to let them drink immediately after we removed their harness. Although we did not know but that this was an old wife's tale, we carefully adhered to this rule. None of our horses ever became lame.

On one occasion the horses' sense, that the day was or should have been done, led to a calamity for which I deserve full credit. Under Bill's leadership we sought to make the acreage across the railroad tracks to be productive and past the swamp. It was poor soil and the forest brush threatened to engulf it. We cleared the minor brush and turned the soil for planting field corn. Although the corn did not thrive, it was worth harvesting as silage. After cutting it by hand we would load it onto a hay wagon for the trip back across the tracks to the barn. As the youngest I was relegated to driving the horses. It was almost time to quit when on the last turn the horses saw the path home and sensed it was time to go there. Maybe they were spooked. Regardless, they bolted down the road. I bailed out. I was not strong enough to yank them to a halt and fearing for my demise I jumped off the wagon. Although I probably could have held on for one heck of a ride, it seemed to be the best choice. It was a successful leap. I was okay.

The horses hitched to the loaded wagon were in full-gallop. We chased after them, knowing there would be disaster ahead. There was no gate on this side of the tracks. On the other side the gate would be closed to keep the cows from getting out while we were working the corn field. What would the team do when it hit the gate at full speed? I pictured a smashed gate needing emergency repair. It would not be that bad. To me, though, it was worse. I was embarrassed. It was my fault.

The horses, seeing their path blocked, took a detour—an immediate left turn, off the ramp, into the ditch and against the fence. That is where they were when we caught up to them. The rear of the wagon was blocking the railroad tracks. If a train was to come by now, before we could move the wagon, we would be in real trouble. Fortunately we could move the wagon just enough for the trains to pass. Bill got the horses free and fixed the fence temporarily.

The next day Bill returned with the horses and towed the wagon back out of the ditch. I blocked the incident from my mind and stayed out of sight.

JBT 01/2007

School for the Eight Kids

One-room school houses were still common when all the children started school. I went to school in a one-room school house, a little over a mile walk down the road toward Lawtons. Walking is how we got there unless the weather was blizzard-like, which in most cases would cause the schools to be closed. If they were not closed, Far would take us in the back of his cattle truck. I attended grades one through six in the one-room schoolhouse when it was finally closed. Later it was converted to a saloon.

I continued and completed my education in Gowanda Central School. Although we lived in the North Collins School District, we carted ourselves off to Gowanda because there was an incident stemming from an ethnic culture clash for one sibling at the North Collins High School. We may have been stuck on the farm on US Rte. 62 and have to live near them, but, to Far, we did not have to go to school with them. (I will leave it to you, to figure who "them" were.) If not going to the school in the district where you lived, the family was required to compensate the school district as it would not receive attendance money. This fee was not required, if the losing school did not offer classes you wished to take. Therefore we sought out classes that alleviated the fee. I do not know if there were any classes to accommodate the girls. The boys had to take Agriculture.

I think Far realized I was not an aggie. So I took Latin. I do not know if Latin was available in North Collins High School. Today, nationwide, Latin classes are rarely available. I distinctly remember Mrs. Schultz challenging me as to what was a Thordahl farm boy doing in her Latin class. My attitude became, "I'll show her." When I became her student with honors, she became my supporter. I also very distinctly remember the North

Collins school Superintendent arriving at the farm unannounced to get his money. Far and I were at work in the yard. Far kept his cool, immediately recognizing the villain and refusing to be denigrated by the local bureaucrat's officious approach, he opened the encounter with, "You'll get your money when its due." Such sacrifice, so little recognized and appreciated at the time.

Otherwise, Niels and Johanne generally had little involvement with the children's school. They never helped them with homework except when it came to writing a personal biography that would be a high school project. It was the only time we were officially told anything about our ancestors.

During our years in grade school, Ma did go with us for the end of year school outing to the beach at Evangola State Park on Lake Erie. I do not recall that they went on the popular school outings to Taylor's Grove just down the road. The seasonal school pageants were attended by all parents who had transportation and could get away. I do not think that Far attended high school graduation ceremonies. They had a party for me that included primarily their card-playing friends. One occasion that must have been a memorable highlight for Niels and Johanne was a graduating-class trip to Washington, D.C. They went with Joan's class, as chaperones. Travel was by train, probably the only train journey Johanne had taken since childhood.

"The Old Schoolhouse"

Just over a mile down the road stood the old schoolhouse, a large square stone building. It was new to me in 1945 when I tagged along behind the older kids as I made that first walks to school. The children from our family and the two neighbors filled half the six grades. The rest of the students were town kids from Lawtons. Lawtons is a small hamlet that had been a trade hub in the early days of Western New York's settlement. Improved transportation would soon pass it by. What would happen to our old schoolhouse?

Starting first grade three months before I would be five years old, I had some misgivings. I eyed the teacher warily as I walked up the entry steps. However, I was sure school was a place of competition, a factor I felt I could handle, regardless of its nature. Sure enough, before the day was through, I was in a fight. It was just part of competition: it was just what I had expected. After pulling me off the much bigger boy, my brothers and sisters assured me there was a limit to competition, and I had exceeded it. It was a lesson that I never forgot.

During recess, we played "kick the can" and "hide-and-seek." Beside the road were large elm trees that made good places to hide. Other trees were used for bases for kick ball and softball. Playing these games I learned, if you did not want to be chosen last, you had to be big or excel in some way. I was a good bit smaller than average. I would try harder; I was determined to compete. If I could not fight, at least I could smack a softball pretty well.

The old school was heated by a large wood burning furnace in the basement. Before school started each cold day, the teacher would stoke the furnace. By the time we arrived, the classroom was adequately warmed. One day we arrived at school to find a large pile of wood to restore our fuel supply.

In secret, Mrs. Stevens asked me to toss the wood through

the window and stack the wood in the basement. Immediately at recess I began my chore. Unbeknownst to the others I was being paid sixty-five cents for this task. They thought I was being punished for something. Being sympathetic they insisted on helping me toss the wood into the basement. How could I tell them that they should not help me because I was being paid? I protested only slightly and doubled my effort to preclude their excess help.

Considering present concepts, techniques, and facilities, the academic environment was pretty basic. In contrast to today's common circular classroom arrangement of tables here were progressive rows of desks. As you moved up to the next grade level, you moved back a row. Off to the teacher's side was a large table for the youngest kids. There was no kindergarten. I still marvel that one teacher mastered the concurrent needs of six grades in one setting. Occasionally, a parent supplemented the standard lessons. She used a Sunday school method to tell stories from the Bible. The simple process of adding felt cutouts onto a felt-covered easel was intriguing as it produced a scene of the story. Try that in today's public schools!

In lieu of academic dedication, I tended to absorb a sense of the times from adult reaction to current events, their conversation and the newspaper. A couple of world events had a profound effect on my life: These events were the Communist take-over of mainland China and the Korean War. Then, there were the presidential elections. In class, I proposed that we could have a pseudo primary election in our school. I made up ballots and listed the names on the blackboard (Chalkboards were made of black slate.): Kefauver, Stevenson, Taft, and others. Of course my favorite won because I had listed his name first and knew the younger graders would select the first name on the list. I am sure the teacher voted for Taft.

Just like the town of Lawtons, progress would soon pass the old schoolhouse by. We no longer had to walk to school. The school district was providing a bus. If the school bus could take students to our school and several other rural schools, the bus could bring them to one central school. Modern transportation was transforming schools all over America. Even if it was a forgone conclusion, it was a public school and its closure must be approved by the people. They must vote on it. Niels and Johanne could not vote. They were not citizens. The names of the voters and the tally can be seen today on the internet. So it was, that my sixth year in the old school would be the last year for old North Collins - District School No. 1.

What was to become of the old school site and its hallmark structure? Its stately elm trees were succumbing to Dutch Elm disease, a scourge that virtually wiped out the elegant elms of New England. Would this grand old building succumb as well? Unused, every building falls into disrepair and is threatened by vandals. Fortunately a young couple came forward with an acceptable offer to buy the property. I would watch as they transformed the old schoolhouse into a stately mansion. No. Instead the enterprising new owners converted our treasured one room schoolhouse into a tavern, an ignominious end for a landmark of learning in my early life.

JBT 10/2005

The whole student body

Character and Culture

Niels and Johanne did not share many Danish customs and traditions with their children, much to the regret of most of them. Generally the children have rationalized that Niels and Johanne wanted them to know the new world which would be theirs. Therefore, they instilled little of their personal treasured customs into our daily lives and shared cultural Danish traditions or customs only rarely for special occasions. Niels and Johanne regularly compared notes between themselves on Danish customs, foods and even religion, usually with little agreement. We were just listeners on these occasions. We always lit candles on our Christmas tree and one time Ma, to our embarrassment, led us around the tree as was an apparent Danish custom. I think most of what I know of our ethnic heritage, I gathered independently and subsequent to my childhood. My siblings often say the same.

One Danish tradition that I had the privilege to observe and enjoy only recently is the celebration of a twenty-fifth wedding anniversary. Niels and Johanne's anniversary, dignified and pleasant, lacked the grand festivities now customary in Denmark for this occasion. It was 2001 when I joined Carl and Anna Jean in Denmark where Leif and Birgit Nohr were celebrating their silver wedding anniversary in typical fashion. After an evening of preparation, with the construction of a symbolic arch covered with greenery and placed over their entryway, the celebration began with an early morning "singing awake" of the couple as all the guests gathered outside their door. The long day continued with a reception in their home followed by a formal breakfast meal at the local inn. Fortunately the tradition includes an afternoon rest period because at early evening a continuous party began with a formal assembly of guests. In a procession that seems automated, every guest greeted every other guest with a hardy handshake and friendly *god dag*. It was a repeat of the morning procession and is a custom that is included at every occasion and learned by children at a very early age—another old country custom that, in our new land, in this less formal culture, was retained only in Niels and Johanne's memories. At the appointed time the guests were ushered into the dinning room at the local *kro* for unending food, drink and entertainment, including singing of songs written just for the celebrants and dancing. The couple, in the first waltz, were joined by all the guests dancing ever closer around them until, trapped by the throng, the husband was restrained while his shoes were ceremoniously, or a bit unceremoniously removed. After a late evening (early morning) serving of coffee and wedding anniversary cake, the end of the affair was told by a serving of soup.

The Danes sure know how to party. More than that they are the most generous hosts ever known, since every time I have visited Denmark (and others have noted the same experience), my hosts have offered places to stay, even giving up their own beds. In 2001 I stayed with cousins Hanne Bjørn, Helge Bjørn, Leif Nohr, and Leif's mother, Gudrun, whose conversation I enjoyed as we bridged our language barrier with pantomime. Niels and Johanne also showed this same Danish generosity throughout their lives.

Niels and Johanne's 30th Wedding Anniversary

Far and Ma never thought to try to guide our future. In fact, for careers they offered no guidance whatsoever, just, to work. Their expectation of hard work was a given, the same as high performance in school was expected. Although their children all did well in school, if a good job could be gained before completion, quitting high school before graduation was not discouraged. Hard work was a hallmark of their child rearing. All the children became wage earners at an early age. The summer of my last school year I worked at the Lawtons Canning factory, a good job with good pay (a dollar per hour) since the year before Eugene had led a strike to increase the wages by 25 cents. By-the-way, Niels did not approve of this striking.

"Picking Beans"

I was a bean picker. No. That is not a euphemism. I was not a cherry picker and I did not pick apples, although I did grapple with a few grapevines and lug a tomato or two in the fall. It was summertime though, when I took up the seasonal pursuit of a buck in the berry patches and bean fields of Western New York. It was a time of plenty and the need for plenty of farm labor, a time just before the complete mechanization of even the delicate task of harvesting a primary local crop—beans.

Before I get to the beans, let me go back to the first dollar I ever earned. Just a couple farms down the road on the way to school was a small patch of strawberries. It was probably a hobby turned commercial enterprise in those new prosperous times after the war. In a day or two, five of my older siblings could pick that whole field. Then one day I got my first chance to join in, an eagerly awaited opportunity. I wanted to earn money like the older kids. I already knew how many baskets I needed to fill to get a dollar, enough to fill a crate, twenty-four. Starting down by the highway the strawberry plants were green and lush, making the fruit harder to find but good size. To make sure I did not miss any ripe berries, my sister would occasionally come behind me to see if I had missed any. She would even add one or two berries to my basket as, after all, they should have been mine.

It was a long day. Moving up the hill as we worked our way down the rows, the plants got thinner and the berries got smaller. However, they were easier to find. I was still working on my first row at the top of the hill when the owner of the patch yelled "Quitting time"—a call I would come to know well. I needed just one more basket to fill my crate. I was frantic; I did not want to quit; I began grabbing at the thin plants that seemed to no longer have any berries.

Then from across the field came an angel. My sister, Joan, who would become known as a champion berry and bean picker, became my champion. She added the few berries from her last basket into mine and then from the meager plants nimbly gathered up enough to fill my twenty-fourth basket of strawberries. From that day on Joan has had a special place in my heart. I was going on six years of age when I earned my first dollar!

That was the last year for that berry patch and for my berry picking for a few years. As child labor in the factories of the industrial revolution was a social issue, about this time child labor on farms became the new cause. At age sixteen you could legally be employed at any job, except some machine operations. Farm kids could do any work on their parents' farm at any age. To us, it did not seem fair. A law was passed that to be employed on a farm you had to be fourteen and have "working papers." Family farmers were not going to take a chance on hiring kids and be severely fined.

About the age of ten or eleven we learned the system, could be trusted to handle it, and were back in the berry patches for a couple farmers who would take the chance. When the child labor inspectors came around, we had two choices: Bluff them with an affirmation that we were quote "picking for ourselves" or hightail it to the woods. More than once we headed for the railroad tracks and then just continued to follow them home. Often the inspector would even suggest that we were, "Picking for yourselves?" . . . We just had to nod. Some might recall that our vulnerability led to exploitation or abuse. There was one farm where we would rather not work.

Back to picking beans: You could make more money picking beans. They are not so delicate as berries so a tight grip and quick pull of a handful of beans filled a bag fast enough. There were more farms with beans and the season lasted longer. One day I was invited to go with the Jentz boys to pick green beans on a more distant farm where they had some connection. The Jentz boys usually did not work away from their farm, a dairy farm, that kept them busy and made them big and strong. Dairy farming was really hard work! Their farmer friend had picked up a truck load of day laborers in Buffalo, something new to me, big black men with bulging biceps and strong backs. Normally, when labor was short, small farms recruited day workers on the Indian Reservation. Large farms had migrant laborers from Puerto Rico who were housed in former chicken coops.

We got an early start; the field was wet with dew; and its size seemed overwhelming. Wally, a year younger than I, and a lot bigger, tore down his row. Robert was also ahead of me in no time. With envy and growing disappointment I imagined the fable of the tortoise and the hare. "Slow and steady wins the race." I was not that slow and I was really steady. By noon I was comfortably ahead of the Jentz boys and saw some of the Buffalo guys lagging a bit too. The sun had done its work, dried the plants and was now beating down. No problem; I fully expected a hot day.

The other workers took breaks. I do not take breaks when I am engaged in manual labor. When I cannot go any further, I just quit; I am done for the day. The day came quietly to an end and I *was not* done! But the owner needed to weigh our effort and take his crew back to Buffalo. I thought I had a chance to have the most weight in my five and one half bags of beans and took it as a compliment when the farmer's wife said, "That's the one with the stones in it." My total was 336 pounds, enough for a ten-dollar day at three cents a pound. A Buffalo man beat me out by six pounds.

Just the same, I came home, a winner. When we sat down for supper, Far asked how much I had earned, and slightly chided my next oldest brother, who had graduated, to an envied workplace—the canning factory. This day I had made more money than my brother. To me, Far's grin was the biggest I had ever seen.

As for that first dollar, some would say I still have it. I'm here to tell you, "It's just not true!" Although I do know where I spent it. Let's just say I saved my money until I could buy a bicycle. I still have that bicycle. So, in a way, I guess you could say I still have the first dollar I ever earned. I still ride that bike too!

JBT 01/2007

The Last Horse Dealer

We had animals which we just seemed . . . to have, but did not have to raise. As Niels would say, he would sell anything, if it made a profit. So most animals did not stick around long. One day a tractor trailer (big truck, a semi) delivered a load of horses from Ohio. The almost empty hay loft was used to tie these horses to the walls, all around, until they could be sold and moved the next day. That was the most number of horses which we ever had at one time.

Niels often traded the stock he had bought at the auctions before he even headed home. It was a most successful rollover-deal. When animals arrived at the farm, it was always a concern for how they would adapt to their new environment. More than once the horses just walked right over the fence, wandered off down the highway and, once or twice, were struck in the dark and killed. Then the dead wagon, a big truck with heavy metal walls, was called and the dead animal was winched by a hind leg onto the pile of carcasses in the truck, an intriguing event for the young children. The dead animals were hauled off somewhere for some purpose unknown, probably to plant where they were converted to fertilizer. I always thought of the destination of the dead wagon as a place far to the south, like, maybe the town of Horseheads—how apropos, the name.

Niels had a contract with the State Hospital about five miles away, a mental institution that had a large dairy farm that provided milk for the institution. When a calf was born, he had to remove the baby within a day. Then he hustled it off to the stockyard in Buffalo where a young calf was highly valued as true veal. After Niels retired and had sold his last truck, he hauled the calves to Buffalo in the backseat of his car. The Hospital dairy farm shut down about this time.

Niels would go to commercial auction places to buy and trade, Sherman on Tuesday, Springville on Wednesday. Before the kids were old enough for school, he would take one or two kids with him where they just hung out all day, usually without a thought to having food or drink. Exciting at first, boring and tiring before the day at the auction was over. On the way home from Sherman, a restaurant stop would be made in Irving where Niels would share a meal with Walter Kaneal, a fellow dealer, a kindly man who weighed more than three hundred pounds. If one of the children happened to be along, they got a treat, a full course meal. I had the best porkchop I ever remember at the "White Horse" and ate every bite like we were always expected to do, regardless of how full we were.

Niels' favorite livestock were the ones he had always known horses. He was successful as a horse and cattle dealer. He went from a one cow truck to a double wide tailgate truck, on which he could load four horses, each facing the side of the truck, with a chain or rope to separate them. We painted his name, phone number, and profession on the doors: Niels Thordahl, Horse and Cattle Dealer, North Collins, NY, Tel. 114F14.

A packed truckload helped to give the horses a steady ride, although work horses, generally, show good balance. To load a hesitant horse he simply took the horse a couple steps back, turned it around a time or two, and then led it straight up the ramp. Apparently by then the horse had forgotten what its issues were. A tougher steed could be blindfolded and, after the traditional turn, it was an easy step onto the truck. We never thought of horses as hugely intelligent beasts, often discussing the old tale how a horse will go back into a burning barn. Loading a cow onto the truck could be more troublesome. Sometimes insisting on going backward, which is exactly what you let it do. Cows are not smart at all.

Niels was good at his trade. He knew horses well and was consistent in his valuing methods. He could tell the age of a horse by examining its teeth. An old horse was "long in the tooth." Lifting a hoof he evaluated their hardiness. To demonstrate how gentle was the horse he was trying to sell, he would have one of his three to four-year-old kids walk under the horse's belly. It was an act that took courage and trust and we gladly performed it with a bit of pride.

One horse Niels happened upon was a beauty, a short stocky draft horse that had an unusual appeal. He even gave the animal a name, the only time that ever happened. Then we entered the horse for show at the Erie County Fair, one of the largest county fairs in America. Joan, the horse, would be awarded a blue ribbon. Joan was then sold. This was the same intent for all his animals. Five years later, when visiting a farm to do business, there was Joan. Niels recognized her right away. I was very sure too. Although it was near the Amish farms, Niels was happy that Joan had escaped a life of working on the Amish farms. Niels stayed away from Amish farm horses. He always maintained that the Amish overworked their horses, thus shortening their working life. He rarely dealt in saddle horses unless he already had a buyer for one.

Some years later, fewer and fewer farms depended on horses. Gas for tractors was cheap and no longer rationed. As the farmers sold their horses, Niels was the dealer who made the best offer or maybe he was the only horse dealer still around. In town after town, as he traveled around the local area he would point out the farm where he bought the last horse in that town.

If there was no demand for work horses, you might wonder what was the market. We understood that in these final days of farm horses that Niels sold them for mink meat, as mink ranches for fur had come into vogue. Mink coats were now affordable to the upper middle class. It's possible that "mink meat" was just a euphemism for horse meat for human consumption, where eating horsemeat was acceptable.

The days of dealing in horses came to end about the time Niels was old enough to retire.

After the Children had Grown

By 1960 the eight children of Niels and Johanne were established in their own lives. Most of them lived nearby, as their parents approached retirement. I had joined the Air Force and was stationed in England. Then tragedy struck as Johanne suffered a paralyzing stroke. After a short time in the hospital, she stayed with Carl and Anna Jean for care until she could return to the farm where Niels became the homemaker and her full time care giver.

They lived comfortably together for only a few more years when Johanne suffered a second, and fatal stroke. Niels sent her ashes to Denmark via the postal system and they were inurned in the Bjørn family plot in Orum, Sdrl. He presented the package to the postmaster in Lawtons, announcing in a voice stifled with sadness, "Here's Mama," as she was also called by friends and neighbors with affection and admiration.

Niels lived for another seventeen years, alone except for periods of travel and when his two surviving sisters, Jenny and Mette Marie, spent the summer with him one year. His travels took him to Mississippi, Kansas, California, and Scotland, on his return trip to America, when he visited me and my family. He regularly visited his youngest brother and best friends in Canada and enjoyed two long trips to Denmark, the land that never ceased being Niels and Johanne's home. He had sold the farm years ago and now yearned for former days.

When his health failed and he could no longer manage to live alone, he entered a nursing home where the inevitable soon occurred. When he died on May 15, 1981, his ashes were sent home where they were inurned next to Johanne's in the Bjørn family plot in the church yard in Orum, Sdrl. Denmark.

Reflections

Niels and Johanne: The Persons They Were

Johanne became a woman in her own right, a dignified lady, a nurturing mother and devout Christian. She was so well liked, tolerant and generous beyond measure. In the early years of television there was a popular show, *I Remember Mama*. Based on the book, *Mama's Bank Account*, it was about a Norwegian immigrant family's struggles in the early twentieth century and how the title character provided leadership. That was Johanne, our mother, to all who knew her personally, "Mama."

Around where we lived Niels was special in a unique way. He wasn't just a father; he was Far, almost like The Far. He was the only man we ever knew who was called Far by his children. There were no other Danes in the area, plenty of European descendants though. They called their fathers dad, papa, and other Anglo names. Children often asked why we called our father, Far—not always in the most polite manner. We may ever have been asked this question before we ever knew that Far was Danish for "father,"—clearly the most significant bit of Danish culture that was bestowed to us.

There was a gracefulness about Johanne. At their first son's wedding Johanne danced with the groom, Carl. Many guests commented how gracefully she glided across the dance floor. Later Ma told me that their accolades for her dancing did not mean she was a good dancer. Rather, good posture, which she attributed to her daily exercise, should be credited. From my insight, I understood that this was the first time she had ever danced in a social setting. I do not know if she ever again danced in her lifetime. Niels never danced.

Marriage at that time was not the partnership it is suggested to be today. There was a biblical sense of obedience anticipated within the patriarchal culture to which they and their friends belonged, Germanic. There was no apparent discussion before decisions or actions were taken. Ma confided in me that there was one time that she "wished she had put her foot down." One of the boys in his mid teens got into trouble for a minor prank. After the sheriff had left the house, Niels told the son to leave also. Later, as a young man, he was welcomed back home without any consolation and lived at home until he married. Although prying a child from the nest in this manner was not unusual at the time, Johanne was not in favor of it.

Ma's maternal compassion shined upon me one night too. While I was still in high school, my unusual pals and I drank a little too much wine. It was the first time I had imbibed—of cheap wine that is. My best friend in high school, Bob Gold, drove my car home. Raymond Smith followed in his car. They helped me to the front door, and I slipped into the house and went straight to bed upstairs. Hearing me retching, Ma came up to check on me. With a tone of disappointment more than concern, she simply said, "You have to try everything." I mumbled a conciliatory, "Never again." It was a vow I wish I had kept.

Johanne was kind, generous and caring. One profound incident stayed with her. On a cold winter night, with drifting snow reducing visibility, an unwary driver had gone off the road at the infamous bend in the highway a few hundred feet from the old house. Johanne heard a slight scratching at the side door, not much more than a cat could make, wanting to come in, out of the cold. When she opened the door, she found it was not a cat. Huddled against the door a young man with no shoes or overcoat looked up with pleading eyes, so cold he could barely speak. Johanne and Niels dragged the stranger into the warm kitchen and undoubtedly saved his life. What was disturbing was that Johanne learned from the crash victim that he had first gone to the nearest house, right on the bend, and been turned away. How could anyone not help a fellow human?

Perhaps she sought to repay a kindness she had been shown. Once, shortly after Niels and Johanne had been married they spent a day in the undeveloped suburbs of Toronto. Hiking along a stream, the newlyweds, in gleeful spirit, decided to climb the bank along the stream. It was a sizable cliff, quite barren. At the top of the bluff there was an unanticipated overhang which they could not negotiate. Then they also realized they could not descend safely. A couple of young men happened by and at some risk to themselves extended their hands and hoisted them over the barrier. It was a kindness Johanne never forgot.

Even when there was no extra money she could not say no to the Fuller Brush Man, who, in those hard times, at least tried door to door sales in lieu of seeking a handout. Many a hobo or other man down on his luck knew that the "Missus" at our house would not deny them a sandwich and some milk. Most came walking up from the railroad.

Generosity came naturally to Niels and Johanne, especially as the children matured and the days of hardship were in the past. Niels gave a small plot of land on the southeast corner of the farm to Carl and helped him as best he could to build a house there, about a quarter mile down the road. Niels also lent Ann two thousand dollars to buy her own home in Salamanca. As a graduation gift, he forgave the last two hundred dollars of repayment. Each year he gave a collector item of Danish significance to each child. Most of the children chose the annual Christmas platter by Bing & Grondal or Royal Copenhagen. On one trip to Denmark he returned with paintings on rolled canvas, one for each child. The small framed painting which I received, a classic scene of a Danish windmill on a farm with geese in the foreground, he delivered to me in Scotland on his return trip from Denmark.

Niels could legitimately be described as a rugged individual, headstrong with firm opinions garnered over a lifetime, and he was a stern father. Niels was a learned man with strong opinions and a worldly view, a keen memory and a sharp mind that served him to the end. Although some of his opinions may seem radical today, they were shared by his friends. Among the many men with whom he conversed, in business and as neighbors, there were no arguments. He was also gregarious, at ease in any situation, and, in spite of our seemingly isolated social status, Niels had many friends. He listened to the news and read newspapers and books extensively. After Far finished with the Sunday newspaper, Johanne would take her turn. She did not read much else and rarely shared an opinion on current issues.

Niels had learned English on his first trip to America. Johanne did not have the same opportunity as Niels, until they came to Buffalo. Here, after being in an English-speaking country for a year already, their landlord's teenage daughter, Jean Zeufle, helped Johanne to learn English. Johanne was so grateful that, when her children were old enough to understand her appreciation, she made sure they knew who her English teacher had been. Except that Ma sometimes used a Danish "*dee*" on some words, Niels and Johanne showed no evidence of their native tongue.

Niels received a periodical type paper from Denmark. Certainly the copy with a full page front cover-picture and article of his niece, Grethe Thordahl, starring in Denmark's production of *Annie Get Your Gun*, was a prized edition.

Niels was the family correspondent who wrote quite religiously to many family members in Denmark. Other than those close to him, the only other person with whom he corresponded was a lady friend of mine while I was stationed in England. I do not know how the correspondence started. Through her I learned about his last confrontation with America's government bureaucracy. Far had shared with her, how government agents wished him to concede to a set amount that should be his government pension for which uncertain records of documented earnings could not adequately establish a standard basis. He insisted it be left up to the government and it was.

Johanne wrote to Denmark as well for a long while. Her correspondence fell off dramatically later. The cost of trans-Atlantic phone service precluded even a single phone call to or from Denmark. It could easily have cost ten dollars for one minute. The loss of family members, including Johanne's father, was learned only when ship-transported mail arrived. Later, they sent mail by airmail, which employed the cheapest method available, thin paper envelopes that served as stationary as well. Niels put other standard envelopes, which had been received in the mail, to use as score pads for card games by unfolding the envelopes at the seams. How resourceful is that?

Niels smoked Camel cigarettes, lighting them with "kitchen matches" struck on the dashboard while driving his truck. He had no teeth. Niels was about forty-five when he had his bad teeth pulled and was fitted with false teeth. He put his new false teeth in one time, did not like them and never wore them again. The absence of teeth never changed what he ate though. Apparently to cool hot tea, he transferred his tea from the cup to the saucer and drank it from the saucer.

Johanne and Niels enjoyed the classical music that was common on the radio before the days of television. They never went to movies, although they may have before the family grew so large. Niels mentioned some characters from early movies, Charlie Chaplin and Rosalind Russell. Johanne was inspired by the heroine in *Gone With the Wind*, Scarlett O'Hara, recalling the scene where the heroine tore down the drapes to make an elegant dress to disguise her desperate situation. I think, in her personal life, Ma related to that resigned heroine, a determined woman, an eternal optimist. "Tomorrow's another day!"

Epilogue

Questions, which my niece, Sherri, asked in 2004 caused me to have these thoughts: One could ponder how Niels and Johanne measured their own lives. What were their goals? Did they achieve their goals? Did they feel fulfilled?

I think, because of the example Niels and Johanne showed, my brothers and sisters and I all became hardworking adults, who have been dedicated to our chosen ideals and loyal to our compatriots. It was not a matter of teaching. You just could see the way you ought to be.

In another measure, I have marveled over the last few years how, eight children from a couple in their thirties and beyond, could all have survived to this day, February 24, 2005. I think Niels and Johanne would be pleased for that.

Perhaps, a hundred years from now there will be some, who will look back and say, "They were my ancestors and I am thankful for them and the cultural heritage that they left to me."

Their Eight Children

The birth of Niels and Johanne's eight children spanned eleven years during a period of relocation and transition. The life and experience of each child varied correspondingly.

Carl Bjorn Thordahl

The eight children started in Canada with a son, Carl who was born February 26, 1931 in the Toronto city hospital and baptized there also. He was named after Johanne's brother, Carl, who lived on the island of Bornholm, Denmark. He became a United States citizen in 1969, although he sought citizenship earlier by joining the army. It is sometimes easier to attain United States citizenship by joining the service. Apparently, in peacetime that opportunity had been removed. As children of Danish subjects, all the children would be eligible for dual citizenship until they were twenty-one years old.

Ann Bjorn Thordahl

Their next child was Ann who was born in a hospital in Buffalo, New York on August 25, 1932. Her name was chosen in honor of our grandmother, Ane, who died when Johanne, was only nine years old. The first child of Johanne's stepmother was also named Ane. Ann was often called "sister" as you commonly hear when the second child is a girl after the first was a boy.

William George Bjorn Thordahl

On May 5, 1934, Bill was the first of their children to be born in a Lackawanna, New York hospital. The five children to follow were also born in Lackawanna. Bill, for William, is named after William and George Zuefle, close friends of Far and Ma in Buffalo who assisted the young couple when they first came to America. Naming their children after friends whom they respected was now their chosen way as well as using Anglicized names with the apparent intent to have the new Americans-to-be comfortable in this new land, rather than cling to the old culture that they would know so slightly. The custom of including Johanne's maiden name for their kids was a tradition and show of respect that I think all the children appreciated.

Katherine Joan Bjorn Thordahl

The next girl, always known as Joan was born on July 24, 1935. She was the second child named after dear friends, in this case Kitty Zuefle. George and Kitty Zuefle were affectionately called Uncle George and Aunt Kitty. Kitty is a nickname for Katherine. Thus, Joan was christened Katherine Joan.

Lorne Bjorn Thordahl

Born on June 7, 1937, Lorne was named after Lorne Guy, Niels' first employer in Canada. When Niels first came to North America, he lived and worked in Canada. Lorne Guy was at the dock looking to hire help for his dairy farm and met Niels when he was getting off the boat.

Niels Arne Eugene Bjorn Thordahl

Born on July 29, 1938, Eugene is the only child with his father's name, although he was always called Eugene. Arne was after one of Johanne's brothers. How the name, Eugene, was chosen is unknown.

James Bjorn Thordahl

Two days after her 41st birthday, on November 29, 1940, Johanne gave birth to her seventh child, Jimmy. He was named after Niels' youngest sibling who emigrated to Canada and changed his name to Thordale after having been christened Jensenius Jacob Thordahl and adopted as Brandt. He was always known as Uncle Jim, the family's only close relative in North America. His chosen spelling of Thordale may have encouraged pronunciation more closely to its pronunciation in Denmark.

Edna Bjorn Thordahl

Edna was born at Our Lady of Victory Hospital in Lackawanna, New York on December 26, 1941. She was named after Edna Osborne, one of her godmothers and a close family friend. Johanne's child bearing now came to an end, having given birth to eight healthy infants during the later spectrum of normal child bearing years, without a single complication. She was 42 years old.

The Niels and Johanne Thordahl Family:

Top row: Paul Foster (married to Joan), Bill, Lorne, Eugene, James Easton (married to Ann), Ray Smith (fiancee to Edna).

Second row: Anna Jean (married to Carl), Elaine (married to Bill), Carl, me, Bonnie (one day to be married to me), Edna

Bottom row: Ann, Johanne, Niels, Joan.

Children: Cheryl (Carl's), James on his mother's lap, Dyann (Ann's), Daniel (Ann's), Laurie on her mother's lap, Carleen (Carl's).

Index of Pictures

Printed in the United States
79478LV00005B/43-51